BIBLICAL STUDIES

| Volume 1 |

BIBLICAL STUDIES

by
Peter
J. Gentry

VOLUME 1

Biblical Studies, Volume 1
Copyright © 2020 Peter J. Gentry

All rights reserved. This book or any portion thereof may not be reproduced or used in any manner whatsoever without the express written permission of the publisher except for the use of brief quotations in a book review.

Published by: H&E Academic, Peterborough, Canada
www.hesedandemet.com
Cover design by Kseniia Piddubna

First Edition, 2020

Paperback ISBN: 978-1-989174-48-7
Hardcover ISBN: 978-1-989174-49-4
eBook ISBN: 978-1-989174-50-0

Contents

Preface vii

1. Humanity as the Divine Image
   in Genesis 1:26-28 1

2. The New Israel in Isaiah:
   A Challenge to Covenant
   and Dispensational Theology 25

3. Sanctification under the New Covenant 47

Appendix 71

Preface

Biblical Studies contains further research and study on questions raised by writing *Kingdom through Covenant* co-authored with Stephen J. Wellum.

A group at ETS requested I present on the image of God in 2018. The paper I presented there represents all new research since the publication of the Revised Edition of *Kingdom through Covenant* in June of 2018. All instances of "image" and "likeness" in Hebrew and cognate languages were analysed. In addition, a fresh Discourse Grammar analysis of the Tell Fekheriyeh Inscription was undertaken. The results were integrated with other recent studies of value.

Another group promoting Progressive Covenantalism at ETS requested a presentation for a session in 2018. The essay on the "New Israel in Isaiah" resulted from further research on the inclusion of the nations in the one people of God that is an important thread of the book of Isaiah. Fresh analysis of Chapters 43 and 44, 51 and 52 of Isaiah show that the future restored people of God not only includes the nations but will eventually be called by a completely new name other than Israel.

Finally, a paper on "Sanctification Under the New Covenant" is included. This was a presentation at a Church Symposium in Knoxville, TN. Here I attempted to go beyond the statements given at the end of the chapters on the covenants at Sinai (Exodus) and Moab (Deuteronomy) in *Kingdom through Covenant*. It is one thing to claim that our relationship to God as Christians is not bound by the Old Covenant or defined by it as a package and say that we are under the New Covenant, but what does this look like on a day by day basis in the life of a Christian? I hope the answer is helpful and practical.

Peter J. Gentry
Louisville, KY
November, 2019

1
HUMANITY AS THE DIVINE IMAGE IN GENESIS 1:26–28

So much ink has been spilled debating and discussing the *imago dei*. Can anyone possibly improve our thinking on this topic? Is an attempt to do so arrogance?

Recent study undertaken on the primary sources since the publication of the Second Edition of *Kingdom through Covenant* in June of 2018 has led me to a better grasp and understanding of the ancient texts. I would like to focus here on the consensus in scholarship today and seek to show what can be improved or needs to be altered as far as this consensus is concerned. In the conclusion I shall seek to interpret what this means for human beings and functioning in the world.

Let us note three or four important publications. Some show the consensus existing today while others represent the most recent treatments.[1]

---

[1] Earlier expositions of the *imago dei* by Hoekema and Collins are moving in a direction that is helpful but lack the exegetical precision and sharpening of thought attempted here: C. John Collins, *Genesis 1–4: A Linguistic, Literary, and Theological Commentary* (Phillipsburg, NJ: P&R Publishing, 2007): 61–67 and Anthony A. Hoekema, *Created in God's Image* (Grand Rapids, MI: Eerdmans, 1986).

We begin with the treatment of the Hebrew words *děmut* (likeness) and *ṣelem* (image) in the *Theological Dictionary of the Old Testament (TDOT)*. The articles are by Preuss and Stendebach respectively and derive from the original German publications of 1974 and 1989.² Both scholars assert that *děmut* and *ṣelem* are almost indistinguishable in meaning. Further, they assert that the prepositions *bě* (in) and *kě* (according to) are semantically indistinguishable and are to be understood in the sense of *beth essentiae*. Stendebach concludes,

> in any event, v. 26b is not describing the content of humans being created in the divine image, since although 1:26, 28 do associate this notion with dominion over the non-human part of creation, 5:3 and 9:6 do not. Genesis 5:3 involves a genealogy in which Adam is said to have become the father of a son according to his image. Here the reference to dominion makes no sense. The same applies to 9:6, which justifies the sanctions against spilling human blood by recalling how God made humankind in his own image. Hence dominion over other creatures can only be a result or purpose of being made in the image of God.³

Articles by E. Jenni in *The Theological Lexicon of the Old Testament* derive from an original in German appearing in 1971 even

---

² H. D. Preuss, "דָּמָה *dāmāh*; דְּמוּת *dᵉmûth*," *Theological Dictionary of the Old Testament* (Grand Rapids, MI: Eerdmans, 1978), 3:250–260 and F. J. Stendebach, "צֶלֶם *ṣelem* image, model," *Theological Dictionary of the Old Testament* (Grand Rapids, MI: Eerdmans, 2003), 12:386–396.

³ Stendebach, "צֶלֶם *ṣelem* image, model," *TDOT*, 12:394.

though the English translation came out in 1997 after *TDOT*.[4] His treatment agrees in essence with the results in *TDOT*. The recent commentary of Jean L'Hour may be mentioned.[5] This commentary, appearing in 2016, is over 260 pages and deals only with Genesis 1-2, 4a. It is the most detailed and extensive exegetical treatment in recent scholarship. The results of L'Hour's study are in line with the authors of *TDOT*. In addition, L'Hour considers the Tell Fakhariyeh Inscription, and concludes that *děmut* and *ṣelem* are indistinguishable in this 9th Century BC Aramaic Text. The newer Hebrew lexica, such as the *Dictionary of Classical Hebrew* (2010) and *18th Edition of Gesenius* (2009), do not alter the picture significantly. Finally, in a collection of essays from IVP in 2016, Catherine McDowell popularises her doctoral dissertation published in 2015 and adds material on Genesis 1. She considers *děmut* and *ṣelem* synonymous in both Genesis 1 and the Tell Fakhariyeh Inscription. As we will note later in this chapter, her considerations of the divine image as sonship support the exposition given independently by myself, C. L. Crouch, and Gavin Ortlund[6] in earlier publications. In summary, scholars have generally understood *děmut* and *ṣelem* to be virtually identical in meaning.

---

[4] Ernst Jenni and Claus Westermann, *Theological Lexicon of the Old Testament*, trans. Mark E. Biddle, 3 vols. (Peabody, MA: Hendrickson, 1997), 339-342, 1080-1085.

[5] Jean L'Hour, *Genèse 1-2,4a Commentaire* (Études Bibliques, Nouvelle série 71; Leuven: Peeters, 2016), 166-180.

[6] See also C. L. Crouch, "Genesis 1:26-27 As a Statement of Humanity's Divine Parentage," *Journal of Theological Studies* NS 61 (2010): 1-15 and Gavin Ortlund, "Image of God, Son of God: Genesis 5:3 and Luke 3:38 in Intercanonical Dialogue," *Journal of the Evangelical Theological Society* 57/4 (2014): 673-688.

For the first and second editions of *Kingdom through Covenant*, I felt it sufficient to base my study on the description of the words *dĕmut* and *ṣelem* in Hebrew in the superb monograph of Randall Garr which appeared in 2003.[7] While I continue to hold that the description of Garr is both accurate and even-handed, I learned interesting things from my own exhaustive analysis of these words carried out since the publication of the Second Edition of *Kingdom through Covenant* on June 30 of 2018.

Lexical and semantic analysis is based primarily on three things: (1) context and usage, (2) cognate languages, and (3) ancient translations. Of these three approaches, usage is primary in establishing meaning.

First, *ṣelem* is found in seventeen instances in Hebrew and seventeen in Aramaic in the Old Testament. Setting aside the five occurrences in Genesis 1 and 5, six instances refer to images or statues of idols (Num. 33:52; 2 Kgs. 11:18 = 2 Chr. 23:17; Ezek. 7:20; 16:17; Amos 5:26). Three further instances occur in 1 Samuel 6:5, 11 when the Philistines captured the Ark of Yahweh and suffered from boils and mice. They made images of the boils and mice and put them in the ox-cart that carried the Ark back to Israel. Presumably, these images had an apotropaic value. One instance has to do with an image drawn or better etched (חקק) on a wall, possibly in a relief of some sort (Ezek. 23:14 Qr). Two occurrences in Psalms have to do with images that are phantoms or shadows (Ps. 39:7; 73:20), i.e. images that are abstract and non-concrete.

---

[7] W. Randall Garr, *In His Own Image and Likeness: Humanity, Divinity, and Monotheism* (Culture & History of the Ancient Near East 15; Leiden: Brill, 2003).

DIVINE IMAGE

In Biblical Aramaic, five instances refer to a statue Nebuchadnezzar saw in a dream,[8] eleven refer to an idolatrous image or statue he built for his people to worship,[9] and one case has to do with the expression on his face which is described as "the image of his face."[10] Extensive usage in Akkadian is similar. It refers to an image or statue of a god, king, or general image, to a figurine or bas-relief drawing, to a constellation or one's bodily stature, and beyond that are metaphorical uses.[11] Usage in Ugaritic, all epochs of Aramaic, and later phases of Hebrew are similar.[12] Apparently ṣanam is an Aramaic loanword in Arabic.[13] The word is also attested in Old South Arabic and modern ṣ́heri.[14]

The Septuagint usually renders ṣelem as εἰκών, although εἴδωλον is used in Numbers 33:52, ὁμοίωμα in 1 Samuel 6:5, and τύπος in Amos 5:26.

Turning our attention to the 25 instances of děmut in the Old Testament (not extant in Biblical Aramaic, although the cognate verb דמה is found in Daniel 3:25 and 7:3), aside from three occurrences in Genesis, the bulk of the occurrences are in Ezekiel 1, 8, and 10 where Ezekiel is attempting to describe features in his visions. Sometimes he says x is like y, where the

---

[8] Daniel 2:31(2×), 32, 34, 35.
[9] Daniel 3:1, 2, 3(2×), 5, 7, 10, 12, 14, 15, 18.
[10] Daniel 3:19 (facial expression).
[11] AHw 1078 f.; CAD Ṣ 16:79–85.
[12] See DLU 783 and Comprehensive Aramaic Lexicon (http://cal.huc.edu/).
[13] R. Meyer, J. Renz, and H. Donner, *Wilhelm Gesenius Hebräisches und Aramaisches Handwörterbuch über das Alte Testament*, 18. Auflage (Berlin: Springer, 2013), s.v.
[14] Myer, Renz, and Donner, *Hebräisches und Aramaisches Handwörterbuch*, 18.

word *dĕmut* is used for "like" in English. Occasionally he employs the expression דְּמוּת כְּ.[15] Daniel 10:16 כִּדְמוּת is similar. Rarely he speaks of דְּמוּת כְּמַרְאֵה־ (Ezek. 1:26; 8:2) or כְּמַרְאֵה דְּמוּת־ (Ezek. 10:1) or uses מַרְאֶה as a synonym.[16] The pair of instances in Isaiah (13:4; 40:18) function in a similar way to that of Psalm 58:5. They are abstract and non-concrete. In 2 Kings 16:10 Ahaz saw an altar in Syria and sent his priest in Jerusalem a sketch of the altar and detailed plans for construction (1984 NIV rendering is excellent). The word is used in 2 Chronicles 4:3 to describe what looked like bulls below the rim in the casting of the bronze sea. Finally, Ezekiel 23:15 refers to an etching on a wall. This passage will be discussed shortly.

Cognate is the verb *dāmâ* in Hebrew and *dēmot* in Samaritan Hebrew. The related noun occurs throughout all phases of Aramaic, beginning with the Tell Fakhariyeh Inscription, also to be discussed shortly.[17] A rare occurrence in Akkadian means a "copy"[18] while in Arabic, a freeze-image or statue is signified.[19] An indistinct figure or object is the meaning in Tigrinya, a derivative of ancient Ethiopic.[20] The cognate most significant is Aramaic.

---

[15] Ezekiel 1:28.
[16] See E. Jenni, *Die hebräischen Präpositionen, Band 2: Die Präposition Kaph* (Stuttgart: Kolhammer, 1994), 57.
[17] See Comprehensive Aramaic Lexicon (http://cal.huc.edu/).
[18] AK. *damtu* = copy CAD D 3:74. See Meyer, Renz, and Donner, *Hebräisches und Aramaisches Handwörterbuch* 18 (Berlin: Springer, 2013), s.v. דְּמוּת.
[19] Hans Wehr, *A Dictionary of Modern Written Arabic* (Wiesbaden, 1979), s.v. *duma*.
[20] Meyer, Renz, and Donner, *Hebräisches und Aramaisches Handwörterbuch* 18, s.v. דְּמוּת.

DIVINE IMAGE

The rendering in the Septuagint is usually ὁμοίωμα (14×) or ὁμοίωσις (5×), εἰκών (Gen. 5:1), ἰδέα (Gen. 5:3), and ὅμοιος (Isa. 13:4). Can we learn anything new from these data? Let us address directly the claim made often that *děmut* and *ṣelem* are synonyms or indistinguishable. First, let us observe from the cognate languages that at first glance Egypt and Mesopotamia have only one word for image. Conversely, Aramaic seems to be the only language besides Hebrew which really offers both words in its vocabulary. The term *ṣelem* is a loanword in Arabic and Wellhausen thought *děmut* was an Aramaic loanword in Hebrew. As we will see, in the bilingual inscription from Tell Fakhariyeh, the Akkadian part has only one word for image whereas the Aramaic has two different words. Yet further research reveals that Akkadian employs the words *tamšīlu* and *muššulu*, derived from a root cognate to משל in Hebrew, in a way quite similar to *děmut* in Aramaic and so Akkadian may have the distinction possible in Aramaic and Hebrew that I shall propose. In Akkadian, the word *tamšīlu* means 1. "likeness," "effigy," "replica," 2. "image," "resemblance," "counterpart." It can refer to statues, figurines in magic, buildings or topographic features. The images can be concrete or non-concrete.[21] The related *muššulu* can mean 1. "likeness" or 2. "mirror."[22] There may be more overlap in meaning between *ṣalmu* and *tamšīlu* in Akkadian than *ṣelem* and *děmut* in Aramaic and Hebrew, but a distinction is nonetheless possible, as we shall see.

---

[21] CAD T 18:147-150.
[22] CAD M 2:281.

Second, let us observe that the ancient translators did not normally render *dĕmut* and *ṣelem* by the same terms in Greek or Latin. So, they understood them as carrying a different nuance or meaning, however similar or synonymous they might be. They were not just stylistic variants for the ancient translators.

Thirdly, none of the major lexica or lexical studies observe that Ezekiel is the only biblical book besides Genesis which allows us to see both *dĕmut* and *ṣelem* employed side by side, nor do they make use of that text to determine whether or not the two words have a different nuance or are identical and completely interchangeable.

Is there a difference in the Old Testament between these two words? I would claim there is. The term *ṣelem* normally refers to an image or statue of a god or human person. The emphasis is on how the image or statue *represents* this god or human person to the world. Conversely, the term *dĕmut* focuses on the concept of comparison and likeness. Unlike *ṣelem* in Hebrew or *tamšīlu* in Akkadian, *dĕmut* is never used in the Old Testament of a statue. Instead, the word focuses on the relationship of the copy to the original. Sometimes the word essentially functions precisely the same way as the prefixed preposition *kaph*.

While two words may be synonyms, what does this really mean in linguistic terms? Even when we are dealing with synonyms, we do not think that the field of meaning or usage of the two words is identical or overlaps perfectly. There is usually some slight difference in nuance between the two words.

Let us look at the usage in Ezekiel 23:14–15 where both terms occur together and also in the Tell Fakhariyeh Inscription from the 9th Century BC where both terms are also found.

The text in Ezekiel 23:14–15 is as follows:

14 וַתּ֖וֹסֶף אֶל־תַּזְנוּתֶ֑יהָ וַתֵּ֗רֶא אַנְשֵׁי֙ מְחֻקֶּ֣ה עַל־הַקִּ֔יר צַלְמֵ֥י כַשְׂדִּיִּ֖ים חֲקֻקִ֥ים בַּשָּׁשַׁר׃

15 חֲגוֹרֵ֨י אֵז֜וֹר בְּמָתְנֵיהֶ֗ם סְרוּחֵ֤י טְבוּלִים֙ בְּרָ֣אשֵׁיהֶ֔ם מַרְאֵ֥ה שָׁלִשִׁ֖ים כֻּלָּ֑ם דְּמ֤וּת בְּנֵֽי־בָבֶל֙ כַּשְׂדִּ֔ים אֶ֖רֶץ מוֹלַדְתָּֽם׃

[14] But she carried her prostitution still further. She saw men portrayed on a wall, figures of Chaldeans portrayed in red, [15] with belts around their waists and flowing turbans on their heads; all of them looked like Babylonian chariot officers, natives of Chaldea (2011 NIV).

The word rendered "portrayed" by the NIV means "drawn," "etched," or "inscribed." The term "figures" in v. 14 is the Hebrew *ṣelem* and the translation "all of them looked like Babylonian chariot officers" in v. 15 entails the word *dĕmut*. Contrary to authors of lexica and lexical studies, it seems easy to distinguish *dĕmut* and *ṣelem* in this text. The term *dĕmut* focuses on the relationship of the copy to the original. The term *ṣelem*, however, focuses on how the physical figures or images in bas-relief impacted those who saw them, i.e. the relationship of the copy to the larger world. The impact and power of the images is that they excited lust in the eyes of the beholder so that they sought political alliances with the Chaldeans. This is metaphorically pictured as fornication by Ezekiel.

Next, consider the Tell Fakhariyeh Inscription from the 9th Century BC. Professor Alan Millard provides the English Translation in the well-known collection of texts called *Context of Scripture.* The term *dĕmut* occurs twice and the term *ṣelem* also occurs twice. In footnote 10 Millard states,

> [t]he monument is termed *dmwt'* at two points and *ṣlm* at two others, both words clearly referring to the same stone figure. While remembering that Aram. and Heb. are not identical, this parallel use suggests no significant differences of meaning should be sought between the two cognate Heb. words used in a similar way in Gen. 1:26, 27; 5:3.[23]

This view is affirmed by the recent commentary of L'Hour and also in the lexical studies in *TDOT*.

Closer analysis may cause us to question this orthodoxy. I have subjected the Tell Fakhariyeh Inscription to a careful text-linguistic analysis as modelled by Aaron Schade.[24]

This is important for the literary structure of this text. Macrosyntactic signals clearly mark Focus and Topic and these changes in Focus and Topic correspond to divisions in the text vis à vis the literary structure. As Professor Millard himself recognises, the Tell Fakhariyeh Inscription (hereafter TF) actually represents two inscriptions. The first entails the dedication of an earlier statue; the second involves the rededication of the statue currently bearing the inscription.

---

[23] William W. Hallo and K. Lawson Younger, Jr., eds. *The Context of Scripture*, 4 Vols. (Leiden: Brill, 1997-2018), 2:154, n. 10.

[24] Aaron Schade, "Fronted Word Order in Phoenician Inscriptions," in *Linguistic Studies in Phoenician in Memory of J. Brian Peckham*, Robert Holmstedt and Aaron Schade, eds. (Winona Lake, IN: Eisenbrauns, 2013), 111-137.

The following literary structure is informed by all scholarly work on this text, but describes the text according to its content in simple terms:

Literary Structure of Tell Fakhariyeh Inscription
- A. Dedication
  - Identification   1
  - god Praise   2–6a
  - king Praise   6b–7a
  - king prayer   7b–10a
  - dedication   10b
  - king imprecation   10c–12b
- B. Rededication   12c
  - Identification/(king Praise)   13a
  - king prayer   13b–14
  - dedication   15a
  - god Praise   15b–16a
  - king imprecation   16b–23

The attitude, emphasis, and tone in the rededication is different from that of the initial dedication. In the original dedication, Hadad-Yithi is only king of Gozan; in the rededication he is king of Gozan, Sikkanu, and Azran. Obviously, he has prospered and his kingdom has grown. In the original dedication he was a young king; now he is established in his kingdom and much more powerful. Notice in the original dedication, the majority of the text is devoted to praise of his god. The imprecation section occupies only a couple of lines. In the rededication, only two lines take up his relation to his god and a full eight lines occupy the imprecation section. R. Garr has noted this as well. Most importantly, what scholars have not noticed is that the term *dmwt'* refers to the original statue in the first occurrence and to the relationship of the copy to the original in the second occurrence, while the term *ṣlm* refers to the second version of the statue in both its occurrences. So both occurrences of *dmwt'* focus on the relationship of the copy to the original and emphasise the vertical relationship of king to his god while the term *ṣlm* corresponds to the emphasis in the rededication section on the horizontal relationship of king to his subjects — the majesty and power of the king in relation to his world. Here I am simply adding to the detailed discussion of Randall Garr.

Admittedly the Akkadian version doesn't draw out these distinctions, but the country ruled by Hadad-Yithi was originally Aramaic speaking and only secondarily a vassal of Assyria. So, the Aramaic text is primary vis à vis the Akkadian version. In the Akkadian translation, one instance of *dmwt'* and both instances of *ṣlm* are rendered by *ṣalmu* in Akkadian; one instance of *dmwt'* is not translated.

Pace Preuss, Stendebach and Jenni in *TDOT* and *THAT*, L'Hour, Millard and others argue for no distinction between the terms, Randall Garr however, in a article in IEJ on the Tell Fakhariyeh Inscription and in his three hundred page monograph on the image of God, is more on target when he argues that *dmwt'* emphasises the relation of the king to his god while the term *ṣlm* emphasises the relation of the king to his subjects.[25] Notice that in line 15 of the Tell Fakhariyeh Inscription the king states that he made the *dmwt'* better than what it was

---

[25] W. Randall Garr, "'Image' and 'Likeness' in the Inscription from Tell Fakhariyeh," *Israel Exploration Journal* 50/3–4 (2000): 231–232 and *idem*, *In His Own Image and Likeness: Humanity, Divinity, and Monotheism* (Culture and History of the Ancient Near East 15; Leiden: Brill, 2003), 121–122.

before. In other words, the statue made for the rededication has a better likeness to the original than the first statue had. The sculpture was more realistic and the likeness more recognisable. And *dmwt'* is used to express this rather than *ṣlm*.[26]

The Meaning of the Prepositions "in" and "as"

Before turning to the instances in Genesis, let us consider the meaning of the prepositions *bĕ* and *kĕ*. Earlier we saw that the consensus in scholarship is that the prepositions *bĕ* and *kĕ* are semantically indistinguishable and are to be understood in the sense of *beth essentiae*.[27]

In spite of the fact that the two prepositions are close in meaning, we must not assume that the meaning is identical. Randall Garr is correct to affirm that "the differential marking of each non-obligatory phrase suggests that each phrase has distinct meaning, at least in relation to one [an]other."[28] His careful and thorough linguistic analysis reveals that the

---

[26] The concordance of Old and Imperial Aramaic Inscriptions by Schwiderski lists three instances of דמו and six instances of צלם excluding the occurrences in the Tell Fakhariyeh Inscription (see Dirk Schwiderski, *Die alt- und reichsaramäischen Inschriften, Band I: Konkordanz* [Fontes et Subsidia ad Bibliam pertinentes 1; Berlin: De Gruyter, 2004], 211, 710). For דמו, the instance in *Aḥiqar* 201 speaks of "the colour of his face returning." This is relationship of copy to original. In Kraeling 3, 20f, the signatories guarantee a house corresponding to the original. Finally the Tell-Ḥalaf Altar speaks of the correspondence of the statue to the original. The instances of צלם in *Daskyleion* 1, *Emar Stele* Fragment, *Nerab* 1:3, 6, 12 and *Nerab* 2:2 are all in funerary monuments and focus on the relationship of the copy to the world. The image has power for others.

[27] See E. Jenni, *Die hebräischen Präpositionen, Band 1: Die Präposition Beth* (Stuttgart: Kolhammer, 1992), 84.

[28] Garr, *In His Own Image and Likeness*, 95.

preposition *bĕ* = "in" emphasises proximity while the preposition *kĕ* = "as" or "according to" emphasises something similar, yet distinct and separate. Garr's linguistic analysis is also supported by the exhaustive research of Ernst Jenni, who has produced an entire monograph on each of the three basic prepositions in Hebrew. One volume analyses all 15,570 instances of the preposition *bĕ*, a second all 3,000 instances of *kĕ*, and a third all 20,000 instances of the preposition *lĕ* ("to" or "for") in the Hebrew Bible. Jenni concludes that, in fundamental meaning, *kĕ* stands between the opposition pair *bĕ* (marking an equating relation) and *lĕ* (marking a non-equating relation) as an expression of partial equation (and so also partial non-equation) of the semantic characteristics of two quantifications.[29] Thus, again, *bĕ* indicates something locative and proximate while *kĕ* indicates something similar but distal and separate.

We have already seen that, although the words "image" and "likeness" share similar meanings, each has a different emphasis. In the Tell Fakhariyeh Inscription the word "likeness" focuses on the king as a suppliant and worshipper of his god and communicates sonship. The word "image" focuses on the majesty and power of the king in relation to his subjects. These ancient Near Eastern data confirm and correspond to the use in the biblical text. The word "likeness" (דְּמוּת) in Genesis is closely associated with the creation of the human race, human genealogy, and sonship. It occurs in Genesis 1:26 in the creation of humans and again in 5:1, when this is recapitulated

---

[29] Ernst Jenni, *Die hebräischen Präpositionen, Band 1: Die Präposition Beth* (Stuttgart: Kolhammer, 1992), 11–40; idem, *Die hebräischen Präpositionen, Band 2: Die Präposition Kaph* (Stuttgart: Kolhammer, 1994), 11–12.

under the heading "Birth History of Humankind."[30] The third use is in 5:3 with the generation of Seth. The word "image" (צֶלֶם) is consistently used of man representing God in terms of royal rule. Putting the nouns and prepositions together, humans closely represent God in image, i.e., they actually represent his rule in the world. Humans are also similar to God in performing the action of creating human life, *but not in the same way*. Thus, *bĕ* emphasises a way in which humans are closely like God, *kĕ* a way in which humans are similar, but distinct. This interpretation also explains the reversal of the prepositions in Genesis 5:3. Here Seth shares precisely in the matter of generation and sonship but is only similar and not identical in the representation of his father's image to the rest of the world.

We turn now to Genesis 5:1-3 where we have the term "likeness" twice with the preposition *bĕ* and conversely the term "image" once with the preposition *kĕ*.

This is the book of the generations of humanity. When God created humanity, he made it in the likeness of God. Male and female he created them, and he blessed them and named them humanity when they were created. When Adam had lived 130 years, he fathered a son in his own likeness, after his image, and named him Seth.[31]

---

[30] The Hebrew term *tôlĕdôt* is construed as a heading in the text.

[31] Translation by Catherine McDowell, "'In the Image of God He Created Them': How Genesis 1:26-27 Defines the Divine-Human Relationship and Why It Matters," in Beth Felker Jones and Jeffrey W. Barbeau, eds., *The Image of God in an Image Driven Age: Explorations in Theological Anthropology* (Downers Grove, IL: IVP, 2016), 35. See also her doctoral dissertation: Catherine L. McDowell, *The "Image of God" in the Garden of Eden: the Creation of Humankind in Genesis 2:5-3:24 in Light of the* mīs pî pit pî *and* wpt-r *Rituals of*

Catherine McDowell comments as follows:

> Seth is in some way similar to his father, yet he is not Adam, just as Adam and Eve are like God in some way, yet they are not God. The author gives no explanation of what constitutes the likeness, but the plain reading of the text suggests that Seth resembles his father simply because his father begat him. By analogy, humans correspond to God because God creates them. Thus, this correspondence is intrinsic to the relationship between Creator and created. When read in light of Genesis 1:26–27, to which Genesis 5:1–3 refers, the correspondence the author may have had in mind seems to be that of class. Seth is a human being, not a fish or a sheep, because his father is a human being. In short, to be created in Adam's likeness and according to his image means that Seth was created according to Adam's kind.[32]

Ten times prior to Genesis 1:26 we are told that grasses or fruit trees produce according to their kind or that God created creatures according to its kind/their kind. The implication is first that Seth belongs to Adam's kind as a human being; and second, that some kind of kinship exists between humans and God.

As McDowell notes, the divine sonship of the king in the ancient Near East is an enormous topic. In addition to the examples discussed in *Kingdom through Covenant* to illustrate

---

Mesopotamia and Ancient Egypt (Shiphrut 15; Winona Lake, IN: Eisenbrauns, 2015).

[32] Catherine McDowell, "'In the Image of God He Created Them': How Genesis 1:26–27 Defines the Divine-Human Relationship and Why It Matters," 35.

ṣalmu in Akkadian, she draws attention to passages I did not discuss, but which may possibly support the distinction I am making between "image" and "likeness." Perhaps I may cite her illustrations at length so that nothing is taken out of context:

> Beginning with Tukulti-Ninurta I (1243–1207 BC) the divine-royal relationship in Assyria was expressed in terms of statue manufacture and divine birth. In the hymn from the Tukulti-Ninurta Epic, the king's body is likened to "the flesh of the gods," a phrase known elsewhere in the Assyrian Erra Myth as referring to the wood from which divine statues were made. He was "successfully engendered through/cast (ši-pi-ik-šu) into the channel of the womb of the gods" and, as a result, "He alone is the eternal image (ṣalmu) of Enlil," whom "Enlil raised ... like a natural father, after his first-born son." The combination of birthing and manufacturing imagery is striking. Not only is Tukulti-Ninurta's body likened to a divine statue, but the process of his creation is described both in terms of manufacture and procreation. Peter Machinist rightly concludes that here "image" identifies the physical body of the king with a divine statue. However, in this context, "image" may have been intended as a double entendre, referring to the king both as a "living statue" of the god and also as Enlil's royal son. Although the hymn avoids explicit deification of the king, it certainly leaves the reader with the impression that Tukulti-Ninurta I, unlike any other human being, had a unique and special relationship—which finds its closest analogy in sonship—with the god Enlil.
>
> The opening lines of the Babylonian creation story *Enuma Elish* reinforce the idea that image and

likeness terminology designated sonship. The account begins with the creation of the primordial gods: Apsu and Tiamat beget Lahmu, Lahamu, Anshar and Kishar. Anshar and Kishar then beget their firstborn son, Anu, who is described as the likeness (*muššulu*) of his father. The following line reads, "and Anu begot Nudimmud, his image." Both examples define the father-son relationship in terms of image and likeness: Anu is the *image* (*muššulu*) of his father Anshar, and Ea is the "likeness, effigy, replica, image, resemblance, counterpart, or equivalent" (*tamšilu*) of his father, Anu. Although there are additional texts to which one could appeal, the biblical and extrabiblical examples just noted are sufficient to demonstrate that image and likeness language was indeed used in Mesopotamia to define the relationship of a god to a royal or divine son.[33]

Like Genesis 1:26, "image" is used of the body of the king as a statue of the god. There is a double entendre of divine kingship and sonship in the Tukulti-Ninurta Epic, but the emphasis is on kingship and so the term *ṣalmu* is used. Interestingly, in *Enuma Elish* the term "likeness" (*muššulu, tamšilu*) is used when the focus is more on begetting and sonship rather than on royal status. This is a clear indication of the distinction I am proposing in a cognate language. So the examples adduced by McDowell not only support her general treatment, but also the

---

[33] Catherine McDowell, "'In the Image of God He Created Them': How Genesis 1:26-27 Defines the Divine-Human Relationship and Why It Matters," 40-41. See Philippe Talon, *The Standard Babylonian Creation Myth Enūma Eliš: Introduction, Cuneiform Text, Transliteration and Sign List With a Translation and Glossary in French* (State Archives of Assyria Cuneiform Texts IV; Helsinki: Neo-Assyrian Text Corpus Project, 2005), 33.

finer point made in *Kingdom through Covenant* of the distinction between "image" and "likeness": the word "likeness" emphasises the relation to the original and speaks of generation and sonship; the word "image" emphasises the representation of the original to the world and speaks of royal rule and status.[34]

This discussion can be concluded by summarising evidence adduced in detail in *Kingdom through Covenant*. Nathan MacDonald has recently written on Genesis 1:26 as a text without a context.[35] He points to the narratives in Genesis 2, Genesis 3 and Genesis 4 as further discussion and treatment of the

---

[34] McDowell rightly sees human rule as a result of royal status (pg. 34). Failure to distinguish image and likeness, however, results in perceiving humanity's identity as son of God, but not the covenant relationship between humanity and creation (pg. 35–42). McDowell's discussion of Yahweh as father and humanity as son cites important texts in the Old Testament but does not put them into the metanarrative of Scripture as in *Kingdom through Covenant*. A number of the texts cited are descriptions of those given *Adamic* roles and therefore relate more to the point than McDowell thinks (pg. 39). From assessing the ancient Near Eastern data she concludes, "Humanity is defined both as God's royal "son" and as living "statuettes" representing God and his rule in his macro-temple, the world. I have focused on the former because the connection between image and sonship has received far less attention in the commentaries and the secondary sources despite its fundamental importance for understanding what it means to be created in the image of God" (pg. 42). Thus, she admits focusing on sonship even though she acknowledges humanity royal status. For page references, see Catherine McDowell, "'In the Image of God He Created Them': How Genesis 1:26-27 Defines the Divine-Human Relationship and Why It Matters."

[35] Nathan MacDonald, "A Text in Search of Context: The *Imago Dei* in the First Chapters of Genesis," in D. Baer and R. P. Gordon (eds.), *Leshon Limmudim: Essays in the Language and Literature of the Hebrew Bible in Honour of A.A. Macintosh* (Library of Hebrew Bible/Old Testament Studies, 593; The Hebrew Bible and its Versions; London: T&T Clark International, 2013), 3–16.

meaning of the divine image. He also appeals to Irenaeus, who, in spite of bad exegesis at points, understood the important connection between protology and eschatology. This confirms the approach I have taken.

In *Kingdom through Covenant*, both in the First and Second Editions, I attempted to expound Genesis 1:26-28 in the light of Genesis 2-3, Genesis 5, Genesis 9, Psalm 8 and also Luke 3, Ephesians 4 and Colossians 3.[36] Recent work by Catherine McDowell on Genesis 2-3, and also Gavin Ortlund and Richard Lints focusing on the later texts have developed this further. McDowell's argument for sonship is supported by Genesis 5, but Psalm 8 argues for the idea of kingship as related to the divine image.[37]

Michael Jones, a ThM Student at The Southern Baptist Theological Seminary, recently explored the notion of *fictive kinship* in covenants and we need to focus on this idea to flesh out all that is meant by "image" and "likeness" in Genesis 1:26-28.[38] One aspect of covenant language in the Bible and in the ancient Near East is the use of family language to support the notion of covenant. In the Covenant at Sinai, the language in the Covenant Ratification Ceremony in Exodus 24 clearly

---

[36] See chapter 6 in Peter J. Gentry and Stephen J. Wellum, *Kingdom through Covenant* (Wheaton, IL: Crossway, 2012, 2018).

[37] Gavin Ortlund, "Image of God, Son of God: Genesis 5:3 and Luke 3:38 in Intercanonical Dialogue," *Journal of the Evangelical Theological Society* 57/4 (2014): 673-688 and Richard Lints, *Identity and Idolatry: the Image of God and Its Inversion* (Downers Grove, IL: IVP, 2015).

[38] Michael Jones, "Fictive Kinship and the Heart of Yahweh: How Adamic Sonship Entails a Loving Creation Covenant," Paper Presented February 28, 2018 in 84100—OT Seminar, The Southern Baptist Theological Seminary.

portrays Yahweh and Israel as "getting married." In marriage, we have individuals who are not related by blood but who by virtue of the covenant of marriage are now more closely related than blood relatives. Marriage entails fictive kinship. Fictive kinship explains the communal meal eaten at a wedding and the communal meal on the mountain in Exodus 24. In the ancient Near East you don't eat with humans who are not family. When individuals who are not related by blood get married, the first thing they want to do is to eat together to show that they are now closer than any blood/family ties. This is supported by the research of Scott Hahn in his large work *Covenant by Kinship* and also by the massive data collected by Paul Kalluveettil on terms employed in the ancient Near East and Old Testament for covenant where the exact term covenant is not used.[39] There are many ways of speaking about covenant without using the word. So, many agreements and treaties borrow family language. The Suzerain-Vassal treaties employ the language of father and son. This is to underscore the fact that in a covenant, parties have undertaken commitments and obligations as strong or stronger than family ties. Even the relationship of a king to his subjects is understood in these terms since one of the epithets for king in the ancient Near East is "father."[40]

Genesis 5 clearly features generation and sonship as characteristic of "likeness" and Genesis 1 and 2 features servant kingship as characteristic of "image."

---

[39] Scott W. Hahn, *Kinship by Covenant: A Canonical Approach to the Fulfillment of God's Saving Purposes* (New Haven/London: Yale University Press, 2009) and Paul Kalluveettil, *Declaration and Covenant* (Analecta Biblica 88: Rome: Biblical Institute Press, 1982).

[40] M. J. Seux, *Épithètes Royales Akkadiennes et Sumériennes* (Paris: LeTouzey et Ané, 1967), 33. Cf. CAD A 1:71.

The final passage in Genesis mentioning the divine image is 9:6, where the basis for avenging a human life taken wantonly is the fact that we are made as the divine image. McDowell points out that later in the Torah, avenging blood is the duty of the "nearest relative" so that Gen 9:6 affirms the connection between the divine image and kinship/sonship.[41]

The Meaning of *dĕmut* and *ṣelem* in Genesis

Let us now consider the occurrences of *dĕmut* and *ṣelem* in Genesis in light of the lexical study. Then results of our earlier study can be added to this.

The one and only supreme creator deity announces to the divine council in Genesis 1:26 the decision to make *'ādām*. The adverbial modifiers "in our image," and "according to our likeness" indicate a vertical relationship between humans and God that can be described as obedient sonship and a horizontal relationship between humans and all creation that can be characterised as servant kingship. The preposition *bĕ* indicates that humans represent the creator God in the world precisely while the preposition *kĕ* heading "likeness" shows that our generation is similar but not precise to that of God. As I explain in *Kingdom through Covenant*, God addresses the divine assembly but proceeds to create humans in his own image and likeness and disenfranchises the divine assembly by assigning the ruling function to the humans.

In reporting the execution of the divine decision, Genesis 1:27 employs only *ṣelem* with the preposition *bĕ* because this verse is preparing us for the role of humans in the world. Their

---

[41] Cf. Psalm 9:12-13 (11-12 ESV) where Yahweh is the avenger of blood and also 2 Chronicles 24:25.

royal status will result in representing God's rule among creatures on the earth. Their binary sexuality will equip them to multiply as God planned.

The exposition in *Kingdom through Covenant* argues that ruling is the result of the divine image and not the image itself. It also demonstrates that the image applies to both male and female, since *'ādām* is generic. Furthermore, since the grammar applies to the product and not to the process, the fact that humans are the divine image is not merely a description of their function and role but speaks of human ontology and structure as well. We are hard-wired for relationship with God and with all creatures.

The fictive kinship of "sonship" and the royal status of kingship force us to view these relationships as covenantal. This is crystal clear from the language used in the Bible and in the ancient Near East. Moreover, this exposition is both full-orbed, positive, and rich in describing the covenant relationship between humans and God and far surpasses the shallow so-called "covenant of works" described in covenant theology as Richard Lucas has shown.[42]

---

[42] Richard J. Lucas, "Reexamining Eden: The Creation Covenant in Theological Systems," Paper Presented at the Annual Meeting of the Evangelical Theological Society, November, 2016.

2
THE NEW ISRAEL IN ISAIAH:
A CHALLENGE TO COVENANT AND DISPENSATIONAL THEOLOGY[1]

The theme of Isaiah is the transformation of Zion—how we get from a corrupt and idolatrous Jerusalem in the old creation to a holy (i.e. completely devoted to Yahweh) and righteous Zion in the new creation.

Isaiah's description of the New Zion as a city (geographical location and people) brings a challenge to covenant theology because the community is not mixed. It is also a challenge to dispensational theology because the community is not defined in ethnic, national terms.

Introduction

In an essay on "The Literary Macrostructures of the Book of Isaiah" published in the Wheaton Symposium on Isaiah entitled *Bind Up the Testimony*, I laid out four features key to interpreting the book of Isaiah: (1) the role of text linguistics, (2) the nature of Hebrew discourse/literature, (3) the character of the author, and (4) the nature of Hebrew prophecy.[2] Here I shall

---

[1] I acknowledge with gratitude constructive critique of my paper by David Christensen.

[2] Peter J. Gentry, "The Literary Macrostructures of the Book of Isaiah and Authorial Intent." In *Bind up the Testimony: Explorations*

appeal again to these features and especially to the author's tendency to introduce an idea or topic in a mysterious manner and then to delay further information that enables readers to fully understand the topic until a later point in the discourse.[3]

Isaiah 43
The Creation of Israel: Bringing the Exiles Home

Outline of Isaiah 38-55[4]	
Historical Prologue—Hezekiah's fatal choice	38:1-39:8
a Universal Consolation	40:1-42:17
1. The Consolation of Israel	40:1-41:20
2. The Consolation of the Gentiles	41:21-42:13
b Promises of Redemption	42:14-44:23
1. Release	42:14-43:21
2. Forgiveness	43:22-44:23
b´ Agents of Redemption	44:24-53:12
1. Cyrus: Liberation	44:24-48:22
2. Servant: Atonement	49:1-53:12
a´ Universal Proclamation	54:1-55:13
1. The Call to Zion	54:1-17
2. The Call to the World	55:1-13

---

in the Genesis of the Book of Isaiah, ed. Daniel I. Block and Richard L. Schultz (Peabody, MA: Hendrickson, 2015), 227-254.

[3] Gentry, "The Literary Macrostructures of the Book of Isaiah and Authorial Intent," 232ff.

[4] Adapted from J. Alec Motyer, *The Prophecy of Isaiah: An Introduction & Commentary* (Downers Grove, IL: IVP Academic, 1993), 289. Used by Permission.

NEW ISRAEL

The literary structure of Isaiah 38-55 shows that the return from exile involves two distinct issues and stages. This section looks farther into the future, beyond the judgement of exile, to the comfort and consolation of Israel, i.e., bringing them back from exile. Then the Lord will establish Zion as the people/place where all nations will seek his instruction for covenant justice. This is described in the language of the exodus, implying that the return from the Babylonian exile will be nothing less than a new and greater exodus![5] This New Exodus is also described by the term "redeem" (gā'al), which refers to the duties of the nearest relative. Since by virtue of the Israelite covenant Yahweh is Israel's nearest relative, he will "buy back" his people from exile as he once delivered them from bondage and slavery in Egypt. The return from exile, however, is not a momentary task. The promises of redemption are divided into two distinct events: release (42:18-43:21) and forgiveness (43:22-44:23). Release refers to bringing the people physically out of exile in Babylon and back to their own land; forgiveness entails dealing fully and finally with their sin and the broken covenant.

---

[5] For a discussion of exodus language and themes in Isaiah see Bernhard W. Anderson, "Exodus Typology in Second Isaiah," in *Israel's Prophetic Heritage: Essays in Honor of James Muilenburg*, ed. Bernhard W. Anderson and Walter Harrelson (New York: Harper, 1962), 177-195. This is developed and discussed further in Peter J. Gentry, *How to Read and Understand the Biblical Prophets* (Wheaton, IL: Crossway, 2017), 71-91.

The Redemption of Israel in Isaiah 42:18–44:23[6]

A Physical Redemption (42:18–43:21)	B Spiritual Redemption (43:22–44:23)
a¹ Israel's Covenant Disloyalty Resulted in Exile (42:18–25)	b¹ The Depth of Israel's Sin (43:22–28)
a² Creating New Israel: Bringing the Exiles Home (43:1–7)	b² Creating New Israel: The Nations Included (44:1–5)
a³ The Lord, Saviour and Only God Contrasted with Idols (43:8–13)	b³ The Lord, Redeemer and Only God, Contrasted with Idols (44:6–20)
a⁴ Redemption from Babylon (43:14–21)	b⁴ Redemption from Sin (44:21–23)

The paragraph 43:1–7 is a mighty assurance and promise that Yahweh himself will deliver and rescue his people. It is this ability to rescue and to save that distinguishes him from all idols. The next paragraph is clear and explicit about the redemption: God will free his people from Babylon.

Notice how this paragraph begins and ends by affirming that Yahweh has created and formed Israel as his people. We shall return to this in a moment.

The people are commanded not to fear because Yahweh has redeemed them. The word "redeem" means "to do the duty of the nearest relative." In the *Torah*, the duty of the nearest relative entails a number of responsibilities. First, one must buy back property a relative has had to mortgage because of poverty. Second, one must buy back a relative who sold him or herself into slavery to pay debts. And thirdly, one must avenge

---

[6] Inspired by J. Alec Motyer, *The Prophecy of Isaiah: An Introduction & Commentary* (Downers Grove, IL: IVP Academic, 1993), 326.

the blood of a relative from murder. I have attempted to show that in Exodus 24, by virtue of the covenant ratified between God and Israel at Mount Sinai, Yahweh is Israel's nearest relative.[7]

Verse 2 speaks of the difficulties and trials that the people of God will encounter in the process of redemption. Notice that the text does not say, "If you pass through the waters," but rather "when you pass through the waters." The deliverance, rescue, and salvation which will be accomplished by God is not a deliverance from or out of great trials and tribulations, but a bringing of his people safely *through* these trials.

Verse 2a speaks of the difficulties in terms of flood waters. This and a number of other images in this context are from the exodus; Isaiah is describing a future rescue and redemption using language from God's great deliverance in the past. It is also a reference to Isaiah 8 where the people must choose between the mighty river of Assyria and the gentle waters of Shiloah. Ahaz chose poorly: he chose the mighty river of Assyria which floods Judah up to the neck.

Verse 2b also speaks of fire. Although the first exodus involved passing through the waters, the second exodus will involve being rescued through the fire. Isaiah 1:31 and 6:13 picture the coming judgement as fire.

In verse 3 the name for God is the title given to him in Exodus 20; it is the way he is announced at the beginning of the covenant, in the Ten Words.

Note verse 3b, "I have given..." and verse 4 "I will give..." These verses present a problem for the thoughtful

---

[7] Peter J. Gentry and Stephen J. Wellum, *Kingdom through Covenant: A Biblical-Theological Understanding of the Covenants*, 2nd ed. (Wheaton, IL: Crossway, 2018), 387-393.

Christian, as it may seem crass and unjust that God gives other humans as a ransom for his own people. A comparison though, is being drawn between the original exodus and the New Exodus. In the original exodus, God punished the Egyptians and rescued his people Israel, and could be thought of as giving Egypt as a ransom to release Israel from bondage. Verse 3 is in the past, "I have given..." Verse 4 is future: "I will give..." In the New Exodus God will also give other people, even other nations as a ransom to deliver his people. What is not clearly stated here, but must be remembered, is that Pharaoh hardened his own heart against the Lord and deserved the judgements brought upon him and the false gods worshipped by the Egyptians.[8] In the same way, when God rescues Israel from Babylon, judgements will fall upon the Babylonians. We must not think that this will be unfair or unjust since these judgements will be well deserved by the Babylonians, as other passages in Isaiah already have (13:17-14:2, 21:1-10) and will make clear (46-47).

In verses 5 and 6 God calls the exiles home. The beginning of this section has a narrow and national ring to it: Jacob and Israel are specified in v. 1. The ending has a universal ring to it: "Everyone who is called by my name."

Let us come now to the exegetical problem in this text. Notice how creation language is employed both at the beginning and at the end.

---

[8] God in his sovereign rule promises to harden Pharaoh prior to any narrative introduction of his self-hardening (4:21-24).

43:1
וְעַתָּ֞ה כֹּֽה־אָמַ֤ר יְהוָה֙ בֹּרַאֲךָ֣ יַעֲקֹ֔ב וְיֹצֶרְךָ֖ יִשְׂרָאֵ֑ל

43:7
כֹּ֚ל הַנִּקְרָ֣א בִשְׁמִ֔י וְלִכְבוֹדִ֖י בְּרָאתִ֑יו יְצַרְתִּ֖יו אַף־עֲשִׂיתִֽיו

In verse 1 we have "create" (*bārāʾ*) and "form" (*yāṣar*); in v. 7 we have the same two verbs plus "make" (*ʿāśâ*). How is Yahweh the creator of Israel? Is Isaiah thinking of the creation account in Genesis 1? Or is he thinking of the creation of the nation at Sinai? Note particularly that both verbs are participles in v. 1. In many of our English translations they are rendered as past tenses. Is this justified? Is it possible, instead, that Yahweh is the creator of Israel in another sense—that he is creating a future Israel, a new Israel, through the Second Exodus?

This option is supported by the author's tendency to introduce an idea or topic in a mysterious manner and then to delay further information that enables readers to understand the topic fully until a later point in the discourse. In verse 1 he speaks of Yahweh creating Israel. Then at the end of the section he explains how he will create Israel—by bringing the exiles home. This is supported by the fact that he concludes by using the same creation language, only this time he employs past tenses.

The exiles are described as the "sons" and "daughters" of Yahweh who are scattered to all four points of the compass.

The paragraph 44:1-5 appears to repeat the thought of 43:1-7 but with differences. First let us notice how 44:1-5 has a parallel sequence of thought to 43:1-7. First, as in 43:1-7 we have the identification of Israel. Israel is the Servant of Yahweh. She is chosen by the Lord. She is created or made by Yahweh, she is formed by Yahweh, and he will help her. Second, as in 43:1-7, Israel is given assurance. Thirdly, as in 43:1-7, there is a reason for the assurance: Yahweh pours water on the desert and pours his Spirit on offspring of Israel. Fourthly, as in 43:1-7, the result of help and rescue from Yahweh is the growth of Israel and the nations incorporated into Israel. The second statement explains the first: how will the growth of Israel happen? Answer: by incorporating the nations into Israel.

The last point must be defended since disparate interpretations have been offered. We see a people who are glad to acknowledge their relationship with God. This is expressed in four statements following a pattern of a b a' b' repetition:

a   This one will say, "I belong to the Lord."
b   This one will call by the name of Jacob.
a' This one will write on his hand, "Belonging to the Lord."
b' This one will give the name Israel as an honorary title.

The "a" lines express the notion of belonging; the "b" lines mention folks who seem to adopt the name of Jacob or Israel. Who are these folks? Some scholars believe they are Jews who, during the diaspora, hid their Jewishness; they did not want to proclaim their identity and relationship with the Lord.[9] When God brings about this time of blessing and restoration to the descendants of the exiles, there will be a glad response; they will now be happy to admit they know God and proclaim their relationship to him. A major problem for this interpretation is that writing "belonging to Yahweh" on one's hand as a tattoo would be forbidden by the *Torah*.

---

[9] Cf. John N. Oswalt, "The Book of Isaiah: Chapters 40-66" *The New International Commentary on the Old Testament* (Grand Rapids, MI: Eerdmans, 1998), 167-168.

A better interpretation and one that fits well with the narrative plot structure and storyline of Isaiah is that these are gentiles who adopt Yahweh as their God and Israel as their people. Having a tattoo on one's hand would not be a problem for gentiles.

Once again, note that the forms in verse 2 are participles. Yahweh is the maker of Israel; he is the one who forms and shapes them. The last form is a Prefix Form: "he will help them." Here the future tense clearly shows that Isaiah is not contemplating the creation of Israel in terms of Genesis 1 or Sinai, but as a future event. And this event in the future entails non-Jews who are joined to Yahweh and Israel. In other words, here Yahweh is also bringing the exiles home; only these exiles are non-Jewish. Note how Isaiah 56:8 expresses this: "For the Sovereign LORD, who brings back the exiles of Israel, says: 'I will gather more in addition to Israel,—in addition to his gathered ones.'" Not all exiles coming home are ethnic, national Israelites.

Isaiah 50:10-52:12 and the Creation of a New Israel

First note that 50:10-52:12 belongs to the part of Isaiah 38-55 where the work of the agent of redemption from sin is being described. There is a panel of three poems about the servant of Yahweh as follows:

Outline of Isaiah 49:1-55:13

A1. The Servant's Double Mission: Israel and the World	49:1-6
B1. Comment: Mission to Israel and World Explained	49:7-13
C1. Messages of Comfort to Despondent Zion	49:14-50:3
A2. The Servant Listening and Obedient in Suffering	50:4-9
B2. Comment: Trusting the Servant or Your Own Way?	50:10-11
C2. Messages of Comfort to Respondent Zion	51:1-52:12

A3. B3. The Servant Successful, Sin-bearing and Triumphant 52:13–53:12
         C3. Message of Comfort for Israel and the World   54:1–55:13

Three poems describe the coming king and his work. Each poem is followed by a comment. This is normal for Hebrew literature: first the writer presents the topic and then goes over the topic a second time. Following the comments are messages related to responses to the poems. The first is a message of comfort for a despondent Zion. The second is a message of comfort for those in Zion who are responding. The third message is the proclamation to Israel and to the world of the benefits of the New Covenant based on the death and resurrection of the servant of Yahweh described in Isaiah 53.

Therefore, the passage 51:1–52:12 follows the second poem on the servant (If we count chapter 42 as the first poem on the Servant of Yahweh, then chapter 50 is the third poem on the Servant). Isaiah 51:1–52:12 is a section bringing a message of comfort to those in Zion who are responding in faith and pursuing righteousness.

First, note the use of imperatives as literary/rhetorical markers to indicate the literary structure in 51:1–52:12.

51:1	שִׁמְעוּ
51:4	הַקְשִׁיבוּ אֵלַי
51:7	שִׁמְעוּ
51:9	עוּרִי עוּרִי
51:12	אָנֹכִי אָנֹכִי
51:17	הִתְעוֹרְרִי הִתְעוֹרְרִי
52:1	עוּרִי עוּרִי
52:7	מַה־נָּאווּ עַל־הֶהָרִים
52:11	סוּרוּ סוּרוּ

Note the individual masculine plural imperatives calling the audience to hear / pay attention in an A B A' pattern form the initial paragraph or stanza. Four double feminine singular imperatives follow, addressed to Zion, and describe the future salvation in images from the exodus. Two interludes following the first and third double imperatives are indicated by a double first common singular pronoun and an exclamation respectively. This yields the following outline:

A. The New Zion   51:1–8
   B. The New Exodus 1   51:9–11
      C. Interlude: Challenge to Unbelief   51:12–16
   B'. The New Exodus 2   51:17–23
   B''. The New Exodus 3   52:1–6
      C'. Interlude: Celebration of Good News 52:7–10
   B'''. The New Exodus 4   52:11–12

Within the three strophes of the first stanza, the end of strophe 2 in v. 6 has a disjunctive *waw* with salvation and righteousness split over parallel lines. Then at the end of strophe 3 in v. 8 there is another disjunctive *waw* with righteousness and salvation—the order is reversed—split over parallel lines. Also, at the beginning of the fourth stanza in v. 17 we have the cup of his anger parallel to the chalice cup of reeling and then at the end of the stanza in v. 23 the reverse: the chalice cup of his anger parallel to the cup of reeling.

   The following outline attempts to delineate and describe the content in more detail:

Outline of Isaiah 51:1–52:12

A. Great Promises Engender Hope of Future Salvation   51:1–8
   1. The Past: Rock Quarry of Abraham   1–3
   2. The Future: Torah for the Nations   4–5

	3. The Hope of Righteousness and Salvation	6–8
	a. It Will Outlast the Old Creation	6
	b. It Will Outlast Human Opposition	7–8
B.	Assurance and Comfort	51:9–16
	1. The New Exodus	51:9–11
	2. Comfort for Zion, the Captives, and the Servant	51:12–16
	a. For Zion	12–13
	b. For the Captives	14–15
	c. For the Servant	16
C.	Call to Zion: Begin Exodus	52:1–6
	1. New Zion is Holy, Righteous, and Free	52:1–2
	2. Oppression and Rejection of Yahweh are Over	52:3–6
D.	News of God's Salvation is Fitting	52:7–12
	1. The Good News is Fitting	52:7
	2. The Proclamation of Salvation	52:8–10
E.	Call to Zion: Begin Exodus	52:11–12
	1. Separation from Babylon	52:11
	2. Trust in the God of the Exodus	52:12

Since there is no space for a complete exposition of these verses, we will have to be content to trace themes developed through the section. There is a plot structure developed and moving forward from 50:10–52:12. The development of five different themes may be noted:

1. The Creation of a New Israel (= believing remnant and non-Israelite peoples)
2. The New Exodus
3. The New Creation
4. The Transformed Community Displays Righteousness
5. The Transformed Community Experiences Celebration and Joy

The Creation of a New Israel

In 50:10-11, the final stanza of chapter 50, the Third Poem of the Suffering Servant, divides Israel into distinct and separate groups: (1) those who fear Yahweh and obey his Servant, and (2) those who follow their own insight and understanding, pictured as creating one's own fire and light.

Therefore, in 51:1, those who pursue righteousness includes those in Israel who fear Yahweh and obey his Servant and excludes the rest. Not all ethnic national Israel will be comforted or saved.

In 52:2 the faithful remnant is commanded to consider the rock from which they were cut and the quarry from which they were hewn. As the next verse shows, this is a figure of speech for Abraham, the father of Israel, and Sarah, the one who gave her birth. God called Abraham when he was one person *so that he might bless* him and make him many. What is the purpose of exhorting the remnant to look to Abraham, who was called when he was one?

I suggest the correct interpretation is that this is to give hope to the remnant. God has not abandoned the Abrahamic covenant as the means for bringing blessing and salvation to the whole world. Although Israel is greatly reduced, and nothing like the stars of the night sky or the sand on the seashore in the time of Isaiah, and will be reduced even further, if God did it once (during the time of Solomon—1 Kings 4:20), he can do it again. Therefore, the covenant promise of God and his action in the past is the hope for the future. Isaiah 6:13 shows that the reduction of Israel by fire is so severe one wonders if anyone will be left. This suggests that God might once again raise up his people from one man—the new servant David.

In vv. 4-6, the next strophe of the first stanza, God calls his people to pay attention. *Torah*, or covenant instruction, will come forth from Yahweh and be a light to the peoples. In v. 5 righteousness is paired with salvation: it will arrive as a gift. Yahweh will judge the nations but also save some, for v. 5 ends by affirming that the coastlands will await him and expect his arm. Since the arm is an image of the exodus, this is tantamount to saying that the non-Jewish peoples will be delivered in the New Exodus. Then in v. 6 the former creation fragments and dissipates like smoke and the inhabitants die like gnats. The use of the word "gnats" is a clear reference to one of the plagues against Egypt. But the salvation and righteousness of Yahweh will endure forever.

Verse 7, the third strophe of the first stanza, speaks of those who know righteousness. There is a progression. We began with those seeking righteousness among the remnant. Then gentiles were included. Now we can speak of those who know righteousness. This is followed by one of the most remarkable statements in all of Isaiah: "a people who have the Torah of Yahweh in their hearts." Since the Torah is the instruction in the covenant, this is precisely equivalent to affirming that the people of the New Covenant are a people who, as a community, have experienced the circumcision of heart. The *Torah* of the New Covenant is written on their hearts. This new humanity are not to fear the humanity of the old creation who will be eaten up as moths corrupt clothing, but the righteousness and salvation of Yahweh will last forever.

The New Creation

We do not have sufficient time to discuss all the imagery from the exodus, but let us note Isaiah's creation language in his treatment of the new creation. See how many words from the Creation Account are employed: call (51:2), bless (52:2), multiply (51:2), Eden (51:3), garden of Yahweh (51:3), heavens and earth (51:6, 2×), Canaanite creation myth (51:9), gnats (51:6; exodus is a new creation), maker (51:13), plant (51:13), found (51:13), new heavens and earth (51:16).

Here the doctrine of the new creation is clearly stated. In the middle strophe of the first stanza, in verse 6, the current heavens and earth will dissipate and vanish like smoke. Then, in verses 12–16—a stanza giving encouragement and warning to Zion, the exiles, and the Servant—Yahweh places his word in the mouth of the Servant to plant a new heaven and a new earth. Moreover, at the beginning of this stanza, Zion is accused and challenged because she has forgotten her Maker, the one who created the first heavens and earth. This is a stern warning: the idolaters in Israel have forgotten their Creator. The connection is clear: if one has no doctrine of creation, one has no doctrine of salvation. The significance of this passage in Isaiah is that the new creation and the New Zion are linked: the New Zion consisting of believers from the remnant of Israel and believers from the distant coastal regions who are not ethnically Israelite is, in fact, the new creation. And this new creation is founded and planted by the word Yahweh has put in the mouth of his Servant.

One of the problems in progressive dispensationalism is that their doctrine of the millennium overshadows that of the new creation. Isaiah does not appear to support the theory of mere renovation. The old creation will disappear like smoke; God will make a brand-new world.

The Community Displays Righteousness and Joy

We have noted the progression of thought and plot structure in this section. In 51:3 a new Eden leads to celebration and joy. In 51:8 the old creation wears out, but Yahweh's righteousness lasts forever and leads to celebration. In vv. 9-11 Canaanite creation mythology is used to depict the future exodus as a new creation event. This new creation will end in celebration. In v. 1, "pursuing righteousness" leads to v. 5 where Yahweh says, "my righteousness is near." In v. 7, "knowing righteousness" leads to v. 8 where Yahweh says, "my righteousness is forever."

In 52:1-2, the beginning of the fifth of seven stanzas in this section, we reach a climax of sorts:

> Awake! Awake! Clothe yourself with your strength,
> O Zion! Put on the clothes of your beauty, Jerusalem,
> the Holy City! For no uncircumcised or unclean person will ever enter you again.

These four lines of poetry strike the listener or reader with incredible force.

The paragraph calling Zion to awake in vv. 1-6 contrasts with the second stanza in 51:9-11 calling the arm of the Lord to awaken and the fourth stanza in 51:17-23 calling Zion to rouse herself. The first paragraph is addressed to the Lord and calls the arm of the Lord to awaken and put on strength as in the time of the exodus from Egypt. Deuteronomy 5:15 is one of many, many passages that recalls this: "Remember that you were slaves in Egypt and that the Lord your God brought you out of there with a mighty hand and an outstretched arm." The mighty hand and the outstretched arm are metaphors that became symbols of the mighty display of power in the Ten

New Israel

Plagues and the Crossing of the Red Sea that released Israel from her slavery in Egypt. By contrast, 52:1-6 calls Zion to clothe herself with her strength. There is a cause and effect relationship here. Zion can put on strength because the Lord has put on strength and done what is necessary to release her from slavery, this time from slavery to sin. Now she must put on strength, the strength to get up out of the dirt and come home. Zion is like a child walking along a road that had a muddy section. She stumbled in the muck and the puddles and sat down.

Finally, her father comes and reaches down to lift her up. Now she must reach up and take his hand and pull herself up as he gives her his strong arm. The question is: will she let herself be pulled out or would she rather stay and play in the mud. In 51:17-23 the picture is of a drunk person whose hangover is finished and now they must rouse themselves and get on with life. Here in this text we have a picture of someone imprisoned who is now set free. The question is: will they get up and walk away or will they sit there, satisfied to stay in their filthy surroundings. Jerusalem was called to be a holy city—a community devoted to the Lord. By her undivided worship of the one true and living God, by justice expressed in the way that people treated each other in the community, and by her good stewardship of the earth's resources, she would be distinct from the corruption in the societies around her. In judgement, God has allowed nations and peoples with no understanding of her ways to enter and corrupt her society with different perspectives and ways of doing things so that her community no longer reflects the pattern established for her by God. The question is: does she even want to be free of this defiling situation?

Isaiah speaks of being clothed with strength and beautiful clothes. What do these represent? An analysis of all adjectives, nouns, and verbs in Isaiah dealing with beauty shows that it represents the righteousness of God now given to his people and displayed in human relationships. We can best summarise the data by referring to Isaiah 54:11b-14a:

> Look! I am laying your bricks with black mortar, and I shall lay your foundations with lapis lazuli pavement. I shall hang your shining shields on the battlements like rubies and make your gates like sparkling red jewels. And your perimeter will be special stones, and all your children will be taught by the Lord; and great will be the Shalom of your sons—you will be established in righteousness!

The beauty and strength of the construction of the future Zion pictures the *righteousness* of the New Covenant community. V. 14a explains the vision of the beautiful battlements of the new Zion: "you will be established in righteousness."

Then Isaiah says something absolutely astonishing: no uncircumcised or unclean person will ever enter again the Holy City. In ancient Israel, the person who is uncircumcised represents those outside the covenant community. The unclean person represents the person within Israel who is defiled and unable to enter the temple for worship. Neither one, we are told, will ever enter again. The term "uncircumcised" in this text must either be metaphorical of the circumcision of the heart, or symbolic of covenant membership since we already know that covenant membership is given to non-Israelites. Thus, by the terms "uncircumcised" and "unclean" Isaiah is referring to anyone who is not a member of the covenant community and might defile it from without, or who *is* a member and might defile it from within. And here is the kicker: Jerusalem is called the holy city. The only occurrence of this expression is 48:2, where Isaiah denies to ethnic national Israel the right to call themselves the holy city. Remember that in chapter 1 of Isaiah the faithful city has become a prostitute, a whore. Now she is redeemed and once more we can speak of a covenant community completely devoted to the Lord and characterised by *ḥesed* and *'ĕmet* in all human relations.

Challenges to Covenant & Dispensational Theology

Isaiah's description of the New Zion as a city (geographical location and people) brings a challenge to covenant theology because the community is not mixed. It is also a challenge to dispensational theology because the community is not defined in ethnic, national terms.

Contra Covenant Theology

First, Isaiah's vision of the transformed Zion challenges Covenant Theology because there is no uncircumcised and no unclean person in the city. In fact, the city as such is now holy—completely devoted to God.

Covenant theologians might interpret Isaiah 52:2 by appealing to the "already/not yet" of prophecy and argue that the new creation community described by Isaiah concerns a future point in time. The only problem with such an interpretation is that the seventh stanza repeats, by means of chiasm and inclusio, the teaching of the fifth stanza and Paul cites this text as applying to the church in Corinth:
2 Corinthians 6:17

> Therefore go out from their midst,
> > and be separate from them, says the Lord,
> and touch no unclean thing;

> then I will welcome you

Paul rejects the concept of the church as a community that is mixed and he rejects the concept that when Isaiah speaks of no uncircumcised or unclean person being in the New Covenant community, it is future. Rather, he believes it to be true of the church now.

Contra Dispensational Theology

Second, Isaiah's vision of the transformed Zion challenges Dispensational Theology because the transformed Zion consists of the believing Israelite remnant as well as those of the distant nations who hope in Yahweh. The terms for Israel in Isaiah and the metaphor of trees supports this view.

Terms for Israel in Isaiah

All occurrences of the terms Jacob, Israel, People, City, Jerusalem, and Zion in the entire book of Isaiah have been carefully analysed and considered. Space does not permit a detailed treatment of these here, but the conclusions may be mentioned. The terms Jacob and Israel, especially when paired, almost always refer to *ethnic* Israel. Ethnic Israel seems to be bound for re-creation in Isaiah 43:1 and 44:1. The term "people" in the singular, and especially in the expression "my people" moves from referring to ethnic Israel to including gentile nations. Jerusalem frequently refers to the physical city or the rebuilding of it. Zion speaks of the city in terms of its people, and this is in transformation in Isaiah. It changes from referring to ethnic Israel to referring to a transformed populace that includes believing folks from both Israel and the nations.

The Servant of Yahweh discussed in the poems in 49, 50, and 53 produces the servants—in the plural—in 54:17. By the end of Isaiah, in chapter 65, these servants are contrasted with unbelieving *ethnic* Israel (65:13-16).

Finally, in a number of places, the transformation of Zion stretches language so that Isaiah announces that the creation of future Israel will be given another name or a new name (1:26, 58:12, 60:14, 62:2, 4, 12, 65:15). This in contrast to claims by ethnic national Israel to be the real Israel in 48:1-2.

Trees as Metaphor of Kings and Kingdoms

Kingdoms in the Old Testament are pictured as stately, tall trees. Although the vine comes from Isaiah, the olive tree in Romans 11 comes from Jeremiah.[10] Especially in Isaiah 5-12, the Lord is chopping down trees, including Israel (9:14, 10:14-34). Yet there are New Exodus promises here as well (10:20-27). After the Lord chops down his people, a shoot comes from the stump of Jesse (11:1). This is not another David but a new David. This root in Isaiah 53 bears the sins of many.[11]

Conclusion

In summary, Paul's treatment in Romans 11 is probably derived from Isaiah. Kingdoms in the Old Testament are pictured as stately, tall trees. Although the vine comes from Isaiah, the

---

[10] See Gentry and Wellum, *Kingdom through Covenant*, 2nd ed., 541-543. Our research has been confirmed by William R. Osborne, "Trees and Kings: A Comparative Analysis of Tree Imagery in Israel's Prophetic Tradition and the Ancient Near East" *Bulletin for Biblical Research Supplement* 18 (Winona Lake: Eisenbrauns, 2018).

[11] Cf. Isaiah 11:1, 10; 27:6; 37:31-32; 53:2 (esp.). Ezekiel sees a cedar planted in place of the vine (Ezekiel 16:3, 17:6-9, 22-24).

olive tree comes from Jeremiah. Nonetheless, the idea that Israelite branches are broken off and non-Israelites branches are grafted in nicely sums up the flow of thought in Isaiah. Depending on one's interpretation of Romans 11, there may well be branches of ethnic Israel grafted back in, but they will be grafted into a city or kingdom that contains both Jew and non-Jew.

3

SANCTIFICATION UNDER THE NEW COVENANT

The deliverance or salvation of a human person, according to the Apostle Paul, entails three stages: (1) justification, (2) sanctification, and (3) glorification. While justification and glorification mark the beginning and end points, respectively, of this work of God in a human individual, sanctification refers to the process in between the beginning and the end.

First, I shall devote attention to characterising sanctification. What is meant by this term in the New Testament, and how is this work of God situated in the plot-line of Scripture? We shall see that the place of sanctification in the larger story of Scripture leads to a major problem.

Second, we shall consider the dilemma involved in defining what is entailed by sanctification under the New Covenant, since our relationship to God is no longer defined by the Old Covenant and since the Old Covenant has become obsolete (Hebrews 8:13). What instructions, then, or what righteousness determines our behaviour under the New Covenant and so empowers and instructs the process of sanctification? Is this righteousness different, for example, from that which is expressed through the Ten Commandments? This question, I submit, is unclear to many Christians and, in fact, is the cause of many, if not most, divisions among believers in Jesus Christ.

The Meaning of Sanctification

The English word "sanctification" is formally a verbal abstract noun derived from the factitive verb sanctify. Verbs ending in "fy" in English are factitive: they denote the causation of a state. To sanctify, then, is to make holy. The morphology in English corresponds precisely to that of the Greek word it commonly translates. The Greek word ἁγιασμός is an abstract noun derived from the factitive verb ἁγίζω (Classical)/ἁγιάζω (Koine) "sanctify" or "make holy." The abstract noun ending in -μός is also related to the adjective ἅγιος ("holy").

So far I have expressed nothing new. There is a problem, however, in the common understanding of the term "holy." Here I can only summarise research done by Claude Bernard Costecalde and furthered by myself.[1]

Since the time of the Reformation, the term "holy" has been connected with two concepts: (1) purity, and (2) transcendence. Theologians claim that to affirm "God is holy" speaks of his purity and transcendence.[2]

Many modern theologians like Hermann Bavinck however, base their understanding of the word "holy" on the research of W. W. Baudissin, whose work, "Der Begriff der Heiligkeit im AT," was published in 1878. Baudissin's meaning came from etymology—the supposed origin of the word.

---

[1] See Claude Bernard Costecalde, *Aux origines du sacré biblique* (Paris: Letouzey & Ané, 1986); *idem*, "*Sacré*" in *Dictionnaire de la Bible*, Supplément (Paris: Letouzey & Ané, 1985), 10:1346-1415; and Peter J. Gentry, "SIZEMORE LECTURES: No One *Holy* Like the Lord," *Midwestern Journal of Theology* 12.1 (2013): 17-38.

[2] See Richard A. Muller, *Post-Reformation Reformed Dogmatics: The Rise and Development of Reformed Orthodoxy, ca. 1520 to ca. 1725*. Volume 3: *The Divine Essence and Attributes* (Grand Rapids, MI: Baker, 2003), 499.

He claimed that the Hebrew root קדש was derived from a biradical root *qd* which meant to cut. From this method he said that the basic meaning was "separate" or "set apart." As a general rule, most biblical scholars and theologians have connected the word holy with the idea of moral purity and, in the case of God, transcendence.

Baudissin's etymology, however, is completely speculative and unfounded. No one with a knowledge of linguistics would accept either his approach or his conclusions. Instead, the best way to determine the meaning of a word is by considering how it is used.

The research of Claude Bernard Costecalde is extremely important here. He carefully researched not only how the word was used in the Hebrew Old Testament, but also in the languages of the countries surrounding Israel. Costecalde demonstrated in a linguistically sound way, that the word "holy" means rather to be consecrated to or devoted to. Instead of referring to separation, it refers to humans being prepared and ready to meet God, and always occurs with the preposition "to" and never with the preposition "from."

The revelation of God as holy and the creation of a covenant people who are holy are connected specifically with the events of the Exodus. The term "saint" is, in fact, an *Exodus* word and indeed Paul's use of it in the New Testament has in view the work of Jesus Christ as bringing about a New Exodus.[3]

One discovers in fact the idea of belonging and devotion connected to the notion of consecration at the beginning of Exodus 19 where verses 5-6, and less evidently 10-15 and 22-24,

---

[3] The connection between the term "holy" and the events of the Exodus will be explored in the calling of Moses in Exodus 3 and the calling of Israel in Exodus 19.

affirm clearly the purpose of God: "You will be my personal treasure (*sglh*, Amorite term) among all the peoples—since all the earth belongs to me—and you will be for me a royal priesthood and a holy nation." Without rehearsing here the details and exegetical issues fully treated in a monograph entitled *Kingdom Through Covenant*, priests are persons devoted solely to the service of the deity.[4] Israel as a nation *qadôš* is given access to the presence of Yahweh and devoted solely to the service and worship of the Lord. Moreover, the statements in verses 5 and 6 are double. First, the call to be a holy nation is parallel to the call to be a royal priesthood, and second, the two designations "royal priesthood" and "holy nation" together constitute an explanation of what it means to be Yahweh's personal treasure. The idea of belonging and that of consecration are closely related in these and following verses.

A holy nation, then, is one prepared and consecrated for fellowship with God and one completely devoted to him. Instruction (תּוֹרָה) in the Covenant is often supported by the statement from Yahweh, "for I am holy."

Costecalde demonstrated in his research that the term "holy" does not speak of separation, but rather consecration or devotion to another. Instead of separation, the term communicated being prepared and ready to draw near and meet God. Since relationship with God is by definition covenantal and also not a parity relationship, it entails faithful loyal love and social justice. Faith and obedience are required. The term "holy" speaks of our devotion and loyalty in the covenant relationship and also our obedience to the instructions in the covenant.

---

[4] Peter J. Gentry, and Stephen J. Wellum, *Kingdom through Covenant: A Biblical-Theological Understanding of the Covenants* (Wheaton, IL: Crossway, 2012).

Seen from this perspective, purity is the result of being completely devoted to the Lord rather than the linguistic meaning of "holy" itself. While God's devotion or "holiness" is not the same as ours—it is much greater—his holiness speaks of his commitment to us. Although God is transcendent, the term קָדוֹשׁ ("holy") is not used to communicate this in the Old Testament. While it is true that "high" and "holy" are collocated in Isaiah 57:15, this verse is, in fact, a back-reference to Isaiah 6. In Isaiah 6 the holiness of Yahweh is his commitment to the righteousness enshrined in the Sinai Covenant and his transcendence speaks of the fact that no one can violate the covenant with impunity: God is sovereign and will back up his covenant stipulations with the promises and threats of Deuteronomy 28. Transcendence and holiness co-exist in Isaiah 6 for different reasons.

This analysis is confirmed by A *Greek-English Lexicon* by Liddell-Scott-Jones.[5] The first meaning given for ἅγιος is "devoted to the gods."

Covenants in the Metanarrative of Scripture

Stephen J. Wellum and I have argued that covenants are the key to the plot-structure of the story of Scripture.[6] Here I shall briefly survey the larger story of Scripture in order to show how the new covenant relates to the Old Covenant and how this perspective determines our understanding of sanctification in the New Testament.

---

[5] H. G. Liddell, R. Scott, and H. S. Jones, *A Greek-English Lexicon*, 9th ed. with revised Supplement (Oxford: Oxford University Press, 1996), s.v. ἅγιος.

[6] Gentry and Wellum, *Kingdom through Covenant*.

Six major covenants determine not only the plot-structure of the Bible as a book, a single literary work, but also identify the key epochs and persons.

Covenant with Creation

First is the Creation Covenant or Covenant with Creation. According to the account in Genesis 1 and 2, humans are the crowning achievement of the creative work of God. In Genesis 1:26 God says, "Let us make humanity in or as our image, according to our likeness." Although the terms "image" and "likeness" are synonyms, each word has a slightly different nuance. Though both clearly communicate covenant relationship, the term "likeness" emphasises the relationship of the copy to the original (its use in Genesis 5:1 and 5:3 denotes generation and sonship) whereas the term "image" emphasises the relationship of the copy to others, i.e. how the copy represents the original in relationship to others. This is connected to ruling in Genesis 1:26-28. These two terms occur in prepositional phrases that are non-obligatory in the clauses in which they occur. The prepositions are similar, but differ in meaning. The preposition *bə* heading the term "image" demonstrates that humanity represents the deity to the world precisely. The preposition *kə* heading the term "likeness" indicates that humanity's creative and generative power is similar, but not exactly the same, as that of the deity. Although the language of generation and sonship is not literal but metaphorical, it demonstrates in the context of the ancient Near East and the Bible that the relationship is covenantal.[7] Later, father-son

---

[7] See further, Gavin Ortlund, "Image of God, Son of God: Genesis 5:3 and Luke 3:38 in Intercanonical Dialogue," *Journal of the Evangelical Theological Society* 57/4 (2014): 673-688.

language is employed in international treaties to communicate the same thing. Language from a covenantal community—the family—is applied to relationships between countries and their kings. Thus, the act of the creation of humanity as the divine image establishes a covenant relationship that is both vertical in relationship to God and horizontal in relationship to the rest of creation on the earth. While God reigns in heaven, his vice-regent rules for him upon the earth. Word-pairs in the Old Testament employed to summarise covenant relationships are *ḥesed* / *'ĕmet* and *mišpāṭ* / *ṣədāqâ*. These are not parity relationships, but entail one greater seeking intimacy, loyalty, love, obedience, and trust from someone weaker. Genesis 2 confirms the exegesis of Genesis 1 by portraying the Man as both king and priest. As humans focus on the priority of worship, they will learn the character and nature of God and go out into the world equipped to properly represent him and his way.

The covenant relationship humanity has with God is quickly violated by disloyalty, unfaithfulness, and disobedience. Humans establish themselves as autonomous, determined to decide for themselves what is right and wrong and choose their own path, unaware that ontology always trumps autonomy: to separate from the creator God is death, not life.

Noahic Covenant
From this point on the culture of human life develops, but also deteriorates as it is characterised by corruption, social injustice and violence. Von Rad, Westermann and Clines have noted a pattern repeated: (1) sin, (2) divine speech addressing the corruption and social violence, (3) grace and favour unmerited,

and (4) judgement.[8] God responds by judging the world and making a brand-new start with Noah. Noah belongs to the humanity deserving judgement, but is given grace. God establishes his covenant with Noah and the obedience of Noah results in God designating him as righteous. When God affirms his covenant with Noah in Genesis 9, Noah inherits the Adamic role of king and priest as the first Man in a new world. The blessing and commands given to Adam are now given to Noah and his descendants, modified somewhat to fit a fallen world. Although the heart of humans is unchanged by the flood, and God would be just to judge every generation, his commitment to creation and the creation covenant will continue by his unmerited favour. The fact that the human race fails after being given a completely fresh start proves that the problem lies in the heart of humans; we are unable to demonstrate loyalty in the covenant relationship with God. So, a new creation does not resolve the problem of the human heart. The family history of Noah ends with divine judgement upon the Tower of Babel and the nations are lost and scattered throughout the earth.

Abrahamic Covenant

The pattern of (1) sin, (2) divine speech, (3) grace and (4) judgement is repeated and the narrative focuses through the family histories of Shem and Terah to Abraham. In Genesis 12 a powerful new word from Yahweh brings forth a new creation from nothing, namely, Abraham and his family as a new Adamic figure who is once again characterised as king and

---

[8] See Carol M. Kaminski, *Was Noah Good?: Finding Favour in the Flood Narrative* (London/New York: Bloomsbury, 2014), 133–136.

priest. The fivefold blessing of Genesis 12:1-3 will reverse the fivefold curse leading from Adam to Babel. God plans to restore his broken creation through Abraham and his family. The blessing will come first upon Abraham and his seed, and then through his seed to all the nations of the world.

The promises given to Abraham in Genesis 12 are enshrined in a covenant in Genesis 15 and the covenant is re-affirmed after the debacle of Abraham's attempt to achieve results through his own strategies in chapter 16. Genesis 17 calls Abraham to adopt the way of Yahweh in the covenant relationship with God. He begins to do this for the first time when he pleads for the rescue of the righteous in Sodom and demonstrates a commitment to social justice. Finally, his faith issues in an obedience that gives ground for fulfillment of the promises and God also affirms his commitment with a mighty oath in Genesis 22.

Mosaic Covenant

When Abraham's family finally grow to become a nation or people, God arranges a covenant with them during the Exodus at Mount Sinai. Here we see that Israel inherits from Abraham the Adamic role.[9] Yahweh refers to the nation as his *son* in Exodus 4:22-23. The divine purpose in the covenant established between God and Israel at Sinai is unfolded in Exodus 19:3-6. As a kingdom of priests, they will function to make the ways of God known to the nations and also to bring the nations into a right relationship to God. Israel will display to the rest of the world within its covenant community the kind of relationships,

---

[9] Exodus 15:17 shows that Canaan becomes for Israel what the garden sanctuary was for Adam.

first to God, and then to one another and to the physical world, that God intended originally for all of humanity. In fact, through Abraham's family, God purposes and plans to bring blessing to all the nations of the world. In this way, through the family of Abraham, through Israel, his last Adam, he will bring about a resolution of the sin and death caused by the first Adam. Abraham and his seed can be viewed as a last Adam because there are no new major starts for the human race as a whole since the beginning of the Abrahamic covenant. Since Israel is located geographically on the one and only communications link between the great superpowers of the ancient world (Egypt and Mesopotamia), in this position she will show the nations how to have a right relationship to God, how to treat each other in a truly human way, and how to faithfully steward the earth's resources. This is the meaning of Israel's sonship.

Deuteronomy, also called the Moab Covenant, is a renewal and expansion of the Sinai Covenant. It is a renewal because the Israel, i.e. the adults, with whom God made the Sinai Covenant, all perished in the wilderness. Deuteronomy is a covenant made with a new Israel and indeed, with all future generations of Israel. It is an expansion, because unlike the Sinai Covenant, it prepares the people for life in the circumstances they will meet in the land of Canaan under a human king.

The Torah or Instruction of Moses, enshrined in the Books of Exodus–Deuteronomy, is considered the Old Covenant by the prophets and by the authors of the New Testament. As well as a positive aspect, there is also a negative aspect to the Old Covenant. The books of Joshua through Kings along with the Prophets and Writings reveal that Israel is not a faithful covenant partner.

In Ezekiel 16, Jerusalem's sins are so terrible in this R-Rated depiction of her crimes that she completely *embarrasses* her pagan neighbours, designated as Samaria and Sodom and portrayed as her sisters. Since Ezekiel is writing after 722 BC, when the Northern Kingdom of Israel fell to Assyria and the people of Israel were deported and foreign peoples were imported to live there, the northern neighbours of Jerusalem constitute the mixed race of Samaritans that resulted from these events. The behaviour, lifestyle, and rejection of Yahweh's Torah by the Samaritans is described and deplored in 2 Kings 17:24–41. The people of Sodom are condemned because an abundance of life's necessities resulted in arrogant independence from God and led to many social injustices. Nonetheless, Jerusalem's acts of covenant violation were so bad by comparison that her sins actually *justified* the conduct of her "sisters," Sodom and Samaria! So, the comparison is not favourable for Jerusalem. The sins of Jerusalem embarrass her pagan neighbours.

Paul explains the situation in Romans 3:19:

> Now we know that whatever the law says, it says to those who are under the law, so that every mouth may be silenced and the whole world held accountable to God (NIV).

Paul is saying that the "law," that is the Covenant at Sinai and Covenant at Moab, was a covenant not made with all the nations of the world, but only with Israel. And yet God holds the entire world responsible for the failure of Israel as covenant-keepers. How can this be just? Well, one of the purposes of the

Old Covenant is to show that even when human beings are given every possible blessing in body, in mind, in spirit—whether in the material world or in the spiritual world—they will not be faithful covenant keepers. So, the entire world is being judged by the example of Israel. It is like playing a game of golf: no matter what handicap you allow the other person, they are never going to win. Israel's failure is, in fact, the failure of all humans: we are lousy at being faithful in a relationship.

Davidic Covenant

Last before the New Covenant is the Davidic Covenant, where God makes a covenant with David and his family line. Exegesis of 2 Samuel 7 demonstrates that the king of Israel was to be the administrator of the Israelite covenant.[10] By depending on Yahweh for military victories, the king would point the people to the kingship of Yahweh. In his rule of the people, the king would represent God's social justice and would also embody the obedience of the people. Thus, kingship in Israel was to be a means of accomplishing Exodus 19:3b–6: the king would be a devoted servant and son of God and would also function as a priest, instructing the nations in the righteousness of God and inviting them to come under the rule of Yahweh.

We see the priestly role of David in that he wears an ephod. The description of David in 2 Samuel 6:14 is identical in the Hebrew text to that of Samuel in 1 Samuel 2:18. We further see the priestly role of the Davidic king in Psalm 110:4. All of this indicates that the king will accomplish in his person the purpose that God had for the nation of Israel as a whole, to be

---

[10] Gentry and Wellum, *Kingdom through Covenant*, 422–427.

a kingdom of priests. The king will embody the nation in himself.

The relationship between the Davidic Covenant and the Abrahamic Covenant is described by various texts in two ways. First, God will use David to bring rest to his people and give them a place. The borders of the land as envisioned in Genesis 15:18-21 are defined in Deuteronomy 11:24 as Israel's "place." 1 Kings 4:20-21 indicates that this geographical "place" belonged to Israel during the time of Solomon, David's son. So, the covenant with David was a means to fulfill the promises in the Abrahamic covenant.

Second, God will use David to bring blessing to the nations as promised in the covenant with Abraham. The covenant with David is the charter or instruction for mankind (2 Sam. 7:19). Psalm 72:17, 132:10, and Isaiah 55:3-4 show how the future king will, by his acts of lovingkindness, be a witness to the covenant and a commander and leader of the peoples as he brings the divine instruction or Torah to all the nations. In fact, he will give his life for the life of his people.

New Covenant

Finally, in light of the failure of Israel to be a faithful partner in the Old Covenant, the prophets announce a New Covenant—beginning with Moses in Deuteronomy 29 and 30. Previous works on the covenants in the Old Testament have tended to deal with the topic of the New Covenant by discussing a number of different passages selected from the prophets and presented *together*. In *Kingdom through Covenant*, the contribution of each of the major prophets (Isaiah, Jeremiah, and Ezekiel) is first considered *separately*. The prophets *do not have a monolithic presentation* on how God will restore things, although variation does not mean contradiction. The contribution of each prophet needs to be considered in the context of his ministry and, especially, within the flow and literary structure of his work. There is also, however, chronological development as Jeremiah meditates upon the prophecy of Isaiah and then Ezekiel reflects upon the work of Jeremiah. When the contribution of each prophet has been heard *separately* as well as *chronologically*, then the multifaceted presentation can be put together into a *whole*. Unfortunately, chronological development was not considered in the first edition of *Kingdom through Covenant*. In addition to discussing passages that treat the topic of the New Covenant, it is important to analyse passages in which a prophet deals with the relationships of the New Covenant to any of the previous major covenants. In this way, the assembling of the biblical teaching on the covenants from the fundamental passages is put together into a superstructure that is derived from Scripture and not from our own imagination or human philosophy.

Here I can only summarise our extensive treatment and highlight a few passages. Isaiah states in 54:13, "All your children will be taught by Yahweh." Note that what is true of the Servant of Yahweh, becomes true for his people. In the Third Poem of the Servant, 50:4, we see that "the Sovereign Lord has given me the tongue of *disciples/learners*, to know how to comfort the weary with a word. He awakens in the morning; in the morning he awakens for me an ear to hear like the *disciples/learners*." Just as the Servant is a *learner,* so his followers become *learners*. And the Servant in the singular, becomes the servants in the plural in 54:17. Isaiah does not describe in detail how the instruction will be given, but clues can be found. In 30:19–21 we find an interesting statement:

> People of Zion, who live in Jerusalem, you will weep
> no more. How gracious he will be when you cry for
> help! As soon as he hears, he will answer you. [20] Alt-
> hough the Lord gives you the bread of adversity and
> the water of affliction, your Teacher will be hidden
> no more; with your own eyes you will see your teach-
> ers. [21] Whether you turn to the right or to the left,
> your ears will hear a voice behind you, saying, "This
> is the way; walk in it."

The word "your teachers" occurs twice in the text. The ESV has the word "teacher" in the first instance and the pronoun "them" in the second. One may interpret the plural as an honorific plural and translate "Teacher" with a capital T, at least in the first instance, since the term is the subject of a verb in the singular. Thus, the Teacher is Yahweh himself.

In 51:7 Isaiah describes the community of the new Zion, which contains both ethnic Israelites and ethnic non-Israelites as a community that has the instruction, or Torah, of Yahweh in their heart(s). This is a clear sign of the circumcision of the heart and shows that Yahweh has placed his instruction within the emotions/minds/wills of his future people.

Nonetheless, these clues call for clarification and explanation. When we come to Jeremiah's passage on the New Covenant in Jeremiah 31 and 32, we see that God will place his instruction in the hearts of his people. This is clearly stated in 31:33-34 and not just something that may be insinuated as in Isaiah:

> "For this is the covenant that I shall make with the
> house of Israel after those days," declares Yahweh,
> "I shall put my instruction within them and upon
> their hearts I shall write it, and I will be their God and

they will be my people. And they will no longer teach each one his neighbour or relative, saying, 'Know Yahweh,' for all of them will know me, from the most insignificant to the most important," declares Yahweh, "for I shall forgive their wrong-doings, and their sins I shall remember no more."

Jeremiah's prophecy here must be interpreted in the light of his earlier oracle in chapter 3:

"In those days, when your numbers have increased greatly in the land," declares the Lord, "people will no longer say, 'The ark of the covenant of the Lord.' It will never enter their minds or be remembered; it will not be missed, nor will another one be made" (NIV).

Why will there be no ark in the future? Because the covenant document will not be recorded on stone tablets and kept in a box in the Temple, but rather written on human minds and wills as humans are built into a temple of living stones.

Even with the prophecy of Jeremiah there is more to be explained. One can imagine Ezekiel sitting there wondering how God will actually write his instruction on human hearts and minds. And so, in his prophecy God gives Ezekiel further light on the subject in 36:26-27 and 37:14:

[26] I will give you a new heart and put a new spirit in you; I will remove from you your heart of stone and give you a heart of flesh. [27] And I will put my Spirit in you and *make* you to walk in my statutes and keep my judgements and you will *do/make* them;

> ¹⁴ **I will put my Spirit in you** and you will live, and I will settle you in your own land. Then you will know that I the Lord have spoken, and I have done it, declares the Lord.

How will God establish his instruction in the feelings/minds/wills of his people? He will place his Spirit in them and cause them to walk in his ways, moment by moment, showing them the path to take.

We have briefly surveyed the sequence of covenants governing the larger story of Scripture. We can now briefly describe the relationship of Old Covenant to New Covenant in order to note problems today in understanding the relationship between the two and then look at 1 Thessalonians 4 which will explain how the Lord's people under the New Covenant receive and follow His instruction and grow in holiness.

The Covenant at Sinai within the Larger Story: The Significance of the Form

Observing the form or literary structure of the covenant as given in Exodus and Deuteronomy is important for a proper understanding of the Mosaic covenant and is foundational for correlating the Old Covenant with the New. The form and literary structure in both Exodus and Deuteronomy show the following points:

(1) The Ten Commandments or Ten Words are foundational to the Judgements or Ordinances and, conversely, the Judgements or case laws apply and extend the Ten Words in a practical way to all areas of life. Nonetheless, one cannot take the Ten Commandments as "eternal" and the Ordinances as "temporal," for both sections together constitute the

agreement or covenant made between God and Israel. It is one package: one cannot accept part of it and reject the other part.

(2) It is common to categorise and classify the laws as (a) ceremonial, (b) civil, and (c) moral, but this classification is foreign to the material and imposed upon it from the outside rather than being derived from the material and clearly marked by the literary structure of the text. In fact, the ceremonial, civil, and moral laws are all mixed together, not only in the Judgements or Ordinances, but in the Ten Words as well (the Sabbath may be properly classified as ceremonial). Those who claim the distinction between ceremonial, civil, and moral law do so because they want to affirm that the ceremonial (and in some cases, civil) laws no longer apply, but the moral laws are eternal. Unfortunately, John Frame in his major work on *The Doctrine of the Christian Life* and Bruce Waltke in his equally magisterial *An Old Testament Theology* perpetuate this tradition.[11] This is an inaccurate representation of Scripture at this point. Exodus 24 clearly indicates that the Book of the Covenant consists of the Ten Words and the Judgements, and this is the covenant (both the Ten Words and Judgements) that Jesus declares he has completely fulfilled[12] and Hebrews declares

---

[11] John M. Frame, *The Doctrine of the Christian Life* (Phillipsburg, NJ: P&R, 2008), 213–217. Frame says, "the distinction [moral, ceremonial and civil law in the Westminster Confession] is a good one, in a rough-and-ready way" (213). Later he admits that "the laws of the Pentateuch are not clearly labelled as moral, civil, or ceremonial" (214). In the end, he struggles to provide clear criteria to show what is and what is not applicable for Christians today from the old covenant. See also Waltke, *An Old Testament Theology* (Grand Rapids, MI: Zondervan, 2007), 434, 436.

[12] Matthew 5:17.

is now made obsolete by the New Covenant.[13] What we can say to represent accurately the teaching of Scripture is that the righteousness of God codified, enshrined, and encapsulated in the Old Covenant has not changed, and that this same righteousness is now codified and enshrined in the new.[14]

(3) When one compares Exodus and Deuteronomy with contemporary documents from the ancient Near East in both content and form, two features are without parallel:

a) in content, the biblical documents are identical to ancient Near Eastern law codes, but do not have the form of a law treatise;

b) in form, the biblical documents are identical to ancient Near Eastern covenants or international treaties, but not in content.

This is extremely instructive. God desires to rule in the midst of his people as king—to direct, guide, and instruct their lives and lifestyle—yet he wants to do this in the context of a relationship of love, loyalty, and trust. This is completely different from Greek and Roman law codes or ancient Near Eastern law treatises, which represent an impersonal code of conduct binding on all citizens and enforced by penalties from a controlling authority. We should always remember that Torah, by contrast, means personal "instruction" from God as Father

---

[13] Hebrews 8:13.

[14] Waltke does say that the Ten Words are an expression of the character and heart of God, but his approach does not provide a biblical criterion for determining how the Old Covenant applies to us today (see Waltke, *Old Testament Theology*, 413). *As a code*, including the Ten Words, it does not apply. The righteousness enshrined in this code, however, is the same that is now enshrined for us in the New Covenant.

and King of his people rather than just "law;" thus a term like "covenantal instruction" might be more useful.[15]

Our view of the Old Covenant is enhanced by accurate exegesis which not only properly attends to the cultural context and language of the text but also allows the text to inform us of its own literary structure and considers the place of the text in the larger story. The biblical-theological framework is especially important because there we come to see the Ten Commandments not merely as fundamental requirements determining divine-human and human-human relationships, but as the foundation of true social justice and the basis of what it means to be a son or daughter of God, an Adamic figure, i.e., truly and genuinely human.

Ephesians demonstrates that just as the righteousness of the Old Covenant can be summarised as "faithful loyal love" to God and fellow humans, so can the righteousness of the New Covenant be summarised this same way.[16] Differences exist between the Old and New Covenants in the detailed stipulations, but not in the content of righteousness.

---

[15] This extremely important point is forcefully made by Waltke in an extended footnote in *An Old Testament Theology* (Grand Rapids, MI: Zondervan, 2007), 405. Nonetheless, it is not properly integrated into his discussion of the relationship between the Old and New covenants.

[16] On Ephesians, see Chapter 15 in the First Edition of *Kingdom through Covenant*, 2012.

The Content of the New Covenant and the Power to Obey Its Instructions
1 Thessalonians 4:1-12

Drawing upon the work of T. J. Deidun,[17] we can now consider a passage in the New Testament which clearly instructs us on holiness or sanctification and correlates the process of sanctification with the New Covenant: 1 Thessalonians 4.

First, Jeffrey Weima helps us to grasp the place of Chapter 4 in the letter as a whole:

> A major shift in the body of the letter takes place at 4:1 as Paul has now completed the apologetic purpose that characterizes the first half (2:1-3:13) and moves on to the exhortative purpose at work throughout the second half (4:1-5:22). The apostle has effectively defended both his past actions during his mission-funding visit to Thessalonica (2:1-16) and his present absence from the believers in that city (2:17-3:10) so that his readers are reassured about the integrity of Paul's motives and conduct and are thus ready to accept the appeals and encouragement he is about to give in the rest of the letter. The apostle has been earnestly praying night and day that he will be able to return to the Thessalonian church and "complete the things that are lacking in [their] faith" (3:10). Since Paul is not able to do this in person, he will do it instead in this letter, addressing the different areas of concern that the just-returned Timothy has reported to him (3:6): the Thessalonian church needs to increase in conduct that pleases God (4:1-12), to be comforted both in their grief over the fate of their

---

[17] T. J. Deidun, "New Covenant Morality in Paul" *Analecta Biblica* 89 (Rome: Pontifical Institute Press, 1981, 2006).

fellow believers who have died before Christ's return (4:13-18) and in their fear over the fate of living believers at Christ's return (5:1-11), and to be exhorted on various matters relating to congregational life and worship (5:12-22).[18]

Outline of 1 Thessalonians 4:1-12

1. Introduction	4:1-2
2. Holiness in Sexual Conduct	4:3-8
General Thesis	4:3a
Exhortations	4:3b-6a
Reasons	4:6b-8
3. Love One Another	4:9-12
General Affirmation	4:9a
Specific Appeals	4:9b-12

Concerning issues that remain, brothers and sisters, we ask you and we urge you by the authority of the Lord Jesus, as you have received instruction from us on how to live and please God, and as you are doing, that you do this more and more. ²For you know what instructions we gave you by the authority of the Lord Jesus.

³ For this is the will of God, your sanctification: that you should avoid sexual immorality; ⁴ that each of you should learn to control your own body in a way that is holy and honorable, ⁵ not in passionate lust like the pagans, who do not know God; ⁶ and that in this matter no one should wrong or take advantage of a brother or sister. Because the Lord is an avenger in all

---

[18] Jeffrey A.D. Weima, "1-2 Thessalonians" *Baker Exegetical Commentary on the New Testament* (Grand Rapids, MI: Baker, 2014), 245.

SANCTIFICATION UNDER THE NEW COVENANT

these things, as we told you before and solemnly warned you. ⁷ For God did not call us to be impure, but to live a holy life. ⁸ Therefore, anyone who rejects this instruction does not reject a human but God, the very God who gives you his Holy Spirit.

⁹ Now about your love for one another we do not need to write to you, for you yourselves have been taught by God to love each other. ¹⁰ And in fact, you do love all of God's family throughout Macedonia. Yet we urge you, brothers and sisters, to do so more and more, ¹¹ and to make it your ambition to lead a quiet life: You should mind your own business and work with your hands, just as we told you, ¹² so that your daily life may win the respect of outsiders and so that you will not be dependent on anybody (NIV 2011).

This part of 1 Thessalonians provides us with a clear picture of Paul's teaching on holiness or sanctification and how the New Covenant is the means for accomplishing this in the life of believers.

First there is a general instruction in v. 3a. Then in vv. 3b-6a instructions that are detailed and specific are given, followed by the reasons for them in vv. 6b-8.

The instructions are given to the believer in three ways. Verses 1 and 2 indicate first of all that the commands and instructions come from the Lord Jesus himself. Second, the commands and instructions come from the Apostles, who are agents of the Lord Jesus. It is clear that they give instruction by the authority of the Lord Jesus.

Third, the instruction in the New Covenant comes to the believer through the Holy Spirit acting directly upon and within each person. This is based squarely on the teaching of the prophets of the Old Testament.

Deidun demonstrates decisively that the phrase "God, who gives his Holy Spirit to you" in v. 8b comes directly from Ezekiel 36:36 and the phrase "you yourselves have been taught by God" is based directly upon Isaiah 54:13. In analysis of θεοδίδακτοι (taught of God) Deidun rightly explains διδάσκειν on the basis of *lāmad* in the Old Testament: "like *lmd* (in *Pi.*) διδάσκειν means to "form" or "train" rather than to "instruct." What is communicated necessarily issues in *action*, for it is addressed not so much to the intellect as to the will; better still, it is addressed to the *whole* man."[19] Furthermore, the syntactic structure of Ezekiel 36:27, i.e. ποιήσω ... ἵνα ποιήσετε, is reflected by ποιεῖτε in 1 Thessalonians 4:10. The syntax of the Greek in the LXX also matches perfectly that in the Hebrew Text: "I will act," says God, "that you may act." Thus to know the Lord, to be taught by him, is to have his Spirit impel the believer to act, and the action specified in 1 Thessalonians 4 is to "love one another."

And what is the content or righteousness of the New Covenant? Is it possible to sum up the content or righteousness in just a few words? In verse 9 Paul commands and instructs them "to love one another." In verse 10 Paul notes that, in fact, the believers in the Church of Thessalonica love all the family of God. The logic of the passage is thus identical to that of Romans 13:9-10:

> The commandments, "You shall not commit adultery," "You shall not murder," "You shall not

---

[19] T. J. Deidun, "New Covenant Morality in Paul," 57 (italics his).

steal," "You shall not covet," and whatever other command there may be, are summed up in this one command: "Love your neighbor as yourself." [10] Love does no harm to a neighbor. Therefore love is the fulfillment of the law (NIV).

As Gordon Fee puts it, "the gift of the eschatological Spirit, [is] the new covenant *replacement* of Torah and *fulfillment* of its righteous requirements.[20]

David Robert Denis, a student at Southern Seminary, submitted a paper on Biblical Theology of the Old Testament, February 28, 2018. The paper was entitled, "The Stylus and the Stone: A Comparison of Covenants and the Noticeable Absence of New Covenant Commands to Write the Instruction of God." He notes that the central command in Deuteronomy 6:4 entailed the members of the covenant community to write out the instructions of the covenant. This was above all, a duty of the king (Deut. 17). But under the New Covenant, there is no instruction to write out the instructions of the New Covenant. Why? Because it is the Holy Spirit who writes the instructions on our hearts moment by moment. Christians are not commanded to write out a list of rules because, as Paul says in 2 Corinthians 3:3, we are Christ's letter, produced by the Apostles, not written with ink but with the Spirit of the living God—not on stone tablets but on tablets that are hearts of flesh.

---

[20] Gordon D. Fee, *God's Empowering Presence: the Holy Spirit in the Letters of Paul* (Grand Rapids, MI: Baker, 2009), 815.

Appendix:
Image of God

After completing the research for Chapter 1, I came across a major work by Andreas Wagner. He is a specialist in ancient Near Eastern studies, and especially art forms. His research confirms in broad outlines the conclusions reached here as can be seen in the following citations from his work. First, Wagner shows how images in the Old Testament, whether physical or verbal must be understood:

> The main thesis of this book is that the image of God's body, as it is drawn verbally in the Old Testament, must be comprehended along the lines of the Ancient Oriental / Old Testament understanding of images. Pictures in our modern world refer to visible objects, they are understood as portrayals of real objects. In the Ancient Orient, pictures referred to objects in their ideal, typical conceived form, more or less independent of their visible aspect. This is combined with a corporeal concept which diverges from ours, in which the body always stands for the functions it exercises. Figures in human form in the Ancient Orient can, therefore, be understood to indicate functions of the body quite independent of visibility, without referring to the visibility of the parts of the body depicted at all. Consequently, verbal images of the body of God in the Old Testament, the anthropomorphic figure, can express the functions connected

with core elements of the body without indicating a visual figure.[1]

Second, here are Wagner's conclusions about the image of God:

> Humans are conceived to "represent." God's cult image ṣælæm is conceived to express similarity, dᵉmût. Together they constitute (a merism) the whole person in his relationship with God. Mankind wields dominion vicariously for God on earth (cf. the mandate to rule), as God's representative (B. Janowski), the mandatary (G. v. Rad). Communication between God and humans must work smoothly if the mandate is to be understood, and therefore similarity is a basic prerequisite. Secondly, humans must be able to act like God, less almighty and within the confines of human ability, but nonetheless capable of acting like God. Both these aspects, communication and the ability to act, lead us back to the similarity of the corporeal and of God and humans, as described previously.[2]

These conclusions are compatible with the conclusions here. Humans are created to have a covenant relationship with God on the one hand and the world on the other. The notions of obedient sonship and servant kingship define humanity both functionally and ontologically. Also, the priority of worship is determinative for implementing the mandate.

---

[1] Andreas Wagner, *God's Body: The Anthropomorphic God in the Old Testament* (London: T & T Clark, 2019), 159. Translated by Marion Salzmann.

[2] Wagner, *God's Body*, 157

About the Author

Peter J. Gentry is Donald L. Williams Professor of Old Testament Interpretation and Director of the Hexapla Institute at The Southern Baptist Theological Seminary in Louisville, Kentucky. He has served on the faculty of Toronto Baptist Seminary and Bible College and also taught at the University of Toronto, Heritage Theological Seminary, and Tyndale Seminary. Dr. Gentry is the author of many articles and book reviews, the co-author of *Kingdom through Covenant* (Crossway, 2012, 2018), and has edited a critical text of Ecclesiastes for the Göttingen Septuagint.

Books by Peter J. Gentry

How to Read and Understand the Biblical Prophets
(Crossway, 2017)

Books by Peter J. Gentry and Stephen J. Wellum

*God's Kingdom through God's Covenants:
A Concise Biblical Theology*
(Crossway, 2015)

*Kingdom through Covenant:
A Biblical-Theological Understanding of the Covenants*
(Crossway, 2012, 2018)

Books by Peter J. Gentry and Christophe Rico

The Mother of the Infant King, Isaiah 7:14
(Wipf and Stock, 2020)

Scripture Index
Old Testament

Genesis
  1:26............................ 10, 14, 16, 18, 19, 20, 52
  1:26–28 52
  1:27 22
  1:26–27 16
  1:26–28 20
  2:5–3:24 15
  5:1 .... 7, 52
  5:3 ..... 2, 3, 7, 10, 15, 52
  5:1–3 .... 15, 16
  12:1–3 55
  15:18–21 59

Exodus
  4:22–23 55
  15:17 55
  19:3 55
  19:3–6 55

Numbers
  33:52 5

Deuteronomy
  5:15 40
  6:4 71
  11:24 59

1 Samuel
  2:18 58
  6:5 4
  6:11 4

2 Samuel
  6:14 58
  7:19 59

1 Kings
  4:20 59

2 Kings
  11:18 4
  16:10 6
  17:24–41 57

2 Chronicles
  4:3 6
  23:17 4
  24:25 22

Psalms
  9:12–13 22
  39:7 4
  73:20 4

Isaiah
  1:31 29
  6:13 37
  11:1–10 45
  13:4 7
  53: 2 45
  27:6 45
  37: 31–32 45
  42:18–44 28
  43:1 44
  49:1–55 33
  50:10–52 33
  51:1–52 .... 34, 35
  52:2 43
  54:11 42
  54:13 70
  55:3–4 59
  56:8 33

57:15 51
Ezekiel
   1:8 6
   1:26 6
   1:28 6
   7:20 4
   10:1 6
   16:3 45
   16:17 4
   17:6–9, 22–24 45
   23:14 4
   23:15 6
   23:14–15 .... 8, 9
   36:27 70
   36:36 70
Daniel
   2:31 5
   2:32 5
   2:34 5
   2:35 5
   3:1 5
   3:2 5
   3:3 5
   3:5 5
   3:7 5
   3:10 5
   3:12 5
   3:14 5
   3:15 5
   3:18 5
   3:19 5
   3:25 5
   10:16 6
Amos
   5:26 .... 4, 5

New Testament

Matthew
  5:17 64
Luke
  3:38 .... 3, 52
Romans
  3:19 57
  13:9–10 70
2 Corinthians
  3:3 71
  6:17 43
1 Thessalonians
  4:10 70
  4:1–12 .... 67, 68
Hebrews
  8:13 .... 47, 65

Biblical Studies, Volume 2
Forthcoming

Name	Date Read

H&E Publishing
www.HesedAndEmet.com

Notes:

NOTES:

NOTES:

www.ingramcontent.com/pod-product-compliance
Lightning Source LLC
Chambersburg PA
CBHW060537080526
44586CB00012B/764